THE GEORDIE GODFATHER

And the Boy from Barnardo's

*To Ray
All the best
" MARIO "*

JOHN "MARIO" CUNNINGHAM

Published by Futures Publications
London, England
www.futurespublications.co.uk

First published in paperback 2009

ISBN: 978-1-871131-18-5

Printed and bound in Great Britain by Tandem Press.
www.tandempress.com

2009 © John 'Mario' Cunningham

Cover design by Tom Lavelle

DEDICATED TO MY BROTHER MICHAEL

CONTENTS

FOREWORD 6

PREFACE 7

CHAPTER ONE – THE PRISON ESCAPE..................................11

CHAPTER TWO – PARENTS FROM HELL 19

CHAPTER THREE – INTO THE ORPHANAGE 24

CHAPTER FOUR – NUMBER NINE...30

CHAPTER FIVE – THE RED JUMPER 38

CHAPTER SIX – THE BLUE ROOM 44

CHAPTER SEVEN – THE BLACK VIRGIN..................................51

CHAPTER EIGHT - SON OF SATAN 56

CHAPTER NINE – THE RELEASE 64

CHAPTER TEN – BORSTAL...72

CHAPTER ELEVEN – THE APPRENTICE 79

CHAPTER TWELVE – MAKING A NAME 85

CHAPTER THIRTEEN – LAST MAN HANGED 95

CHAPTER FOURTEEN – PATCHES 104

CHAPTER FIFTEEN – A PROFESSIONAL VILLAIN 116

CHAPTER SIXTEEN – JOHN THE BARRISTER.....................137

CHAPTER SEVENTEEN – THE GEORDIE UNDERWORLD 145

CHAPTER EIGHTEEN – THE BIGGEST JOB IN THE
                    NORTH EAST 148

CHAPTER NINETEEN – THE BURNING RING OF FIRE 154

CHAPTER TWENTY – LAZARUS – A FRIEND IN NEED 160

CHAPTER TWENTY ONE – MY BROTHER 167

CHAPTER TWENTY TWO – MY BROTHERS AND SISTERS............171

CHAPTER TWENTY THREE – A BAND OF BROTHERS 180

CHAPTER TWENTY FOUR – THE MAN WITH NO PAST...............191

CHAPTER TWENTY FIVE – IS IT NATURE OR IS IT NURTURE? 196

FOREWORD

I first met John "Mario" Cunningham through a friend of mine, George Craig, who told me that he had been asked by John to ask me if I would carry out some research for the book he was writing, *The Geordie Godfather and the Boy from Barnardo's*.

Over several months I looked through newspaper archives and website articles, mainly on the orphanage Mario grew up in, St Mary's Home in Tudhoe, County Durham, and provided them to Mario for his writings.

Mario has always struck me as a personable and affable character with a dry wit and a good sense of humour; he's the type that would help a friend, no questions asked.

He also struck me as the kind of man who could be, if necessary, quite ruthless. He had certainly seen his fair share of carve-ups or fights with some of the biggest names in the criminal underworld from the 1960s right up to the 1990s when he retired from the crime game.

But his story wasn't one of the usual type of true crime tales, focusing on hard cases and anecdotes on crime capers, it was a much more human story and one that goes to the very core of who a man is and how he got where he is.

His story, all his own words, tells what shaped him into the man he is and was and the biggest influence on his life, by far, was his treatment in the orphanage he lived in from the age of four. Like all good stories, there's a twist to his tale.

Some details on Mario's life of crime do feature in this book, but because his time in the crime game was spread over so many years, that will be the subject of a second book which Mario is now working on.

Some profits from this book will go to the Barnardo's charity and after you read it you will understand why.

John 'Mario' Cunningham was a true professional in the crime business, he was one of the few who understood the psychology of crime and the law. But when you read his story you will understand that his life could have been very, very, different.

Patrick Lavelle
July 2009

PREFACE

I have no fear and some people say I have no heart, or at least, if I did have a heart it would be made of stone. I don't react to anything on a human level in an emotional way. I have never flinched in the face of danger, never felt my heart race when confronted by violence or the threat of it and I can never remember ever shedding a tear, even when told of the deaths of family members or 'close' friends. I am not proud of being devoid of any human emotion, in fact I am slightly ashamed of it. I would have liked to have felt, at least a few times, the normal type of human response to fear, stress, the grief of loss, the sadness of bereavement.

Most human feelings, apart from hatred, I was born with and which should have evolved and matured were beaten out of me at an early age in the most brutal, even sadistic, environment, any child could be forced to grow up in. There was a lot more than me who endured the brutality and the never ending psychological torture of being abandoned by parents and, at the most vulnerable and raw age, being thrown into a Roman Catholic run orphanage in County Durham, England.

Within the closeted walls of St Mary's Home in Tudhoe Village the violence meted out to the boys, by those who were supposed to be caring for the youngsters, was relentless and the indoctrination of their fertile young minds *top priority*. The institution would shape the boys of the future.

There is an old Jesuit saying: "Give me a boy until he is seven and I'll show you the man." That philosophy is something that the Roman Catholic religion has fostered and encouraged for centuries in all its institutions. It is a philosophy based on the belief that nurture, rather than nature, makes a person who they are.

In my research for this book I have met up with many of the St Mary's old boys who are now men, like me, in their late 1960s and early 1970s. Virtually all had turned to crime after leaving the orphanage, many serving time at Her Majesty's Pleasure in later life. One or two have lived their lives like recluses, frightened to even leave their homes. There were one or two old boys whose addresses I tracked down whom I couldn't speak to. They had committed suicide.

All these men had been psychologically damaged in some way. Their bodies may not bear the physical scars or bruises from the beatings all those years ago at the hands of the Sisters and Masters of St Mary's, but the emotional damage was etched into their life-weary faces. If I could have gazed into their minds I believe I would have seen the extent of the damage each had suffered and I would have seen that each of them had been touched by evil.

The staff of St Mary's were given these boys, most from broken homes, long before the age of seven ... and in this book I will show you the men.

As for me, my time in the orphanage taught me how to look after myself, but the strongest feeling it left me with was a deep sense of mistrust and hatred for all in establishment, for all those in power, including the police and the judiciary. I also hate bullies and react violently when I see the underdog or the vulnerable suffering any form of injustice.

Looking back on my life now I realise that after leaving St Mary's I was searching for something I had never had ... a family, and within that family I was looking for respect. I found that family in the criminal underworld and in that family I was given respect.

Respect, particularly from other villains, is not something given easily, it is a thing that has to be earned, and I earned it, along with several millions of pounds, during my criminal activities from the 1960s to the early 1990s, across the North of England and Scotland and further afield. My biggest achievement is that I have never had to serve a long prison sentence.

Brian Mills; Mario; Stephen Sayers; Harry Marsden;
Alan Day; nephew, Billy Dixon

In the Geordie underworld I have met and mixed with many of the top names in my time: Harry Perry, Panda Anderson, Billy Robinson, Paddy Leonard, Paddy Devlin, Keith Bell, George "Butchy" Craig, Liddle Towers, and members of some very well known families, including the Tams, the Kellys, the Sayers, the Harrisons and the Abadoms, to name just a few.

Other great friends of mine have included Les Horn, Alan Day, Ted "Machine Gun" Kelly, the Fraser family, Jackie Patterson, Freddie Mills, John Hope, Billy Robinson, Grant Lockyear, Micky Hay, John Loxley, Johnny Bolem, Rob Blackburn, the list goes on. For those I have failed to mention, my apologies.

Mario; Ted 'Machine Gun' Kelly; Michael Sayers; Steve Wraith

I have served time with George Reynolds, who claims to have been a well-known safe blower, with George 'Blower' Shotton, who was a real safe-blower but not in my league, and I was in the cell next to Michael Luvaglio in Durham Jail when he was remanded and later convicted of one of the most notorious murders in the North East and the reputed first gangland style execution.

I will tell you how and why I escaped from Durham Prison; the only man to have ever escaped from the jail dressed as a woman (not because I needed to get in touch with my feminine side!). I will outline my professional approach to crime, the detailed planning and the meticulous execution of jobs which would ensure a large financial return with minimum risk of capture.

My story takes you into places you may never have been before, into the raw underbelly of gangland violence on the streets of Newcastle in the 1960s through to the sudden mysterious disappearances of some familiar faces on the scene, and then out of, it in the 1980s and 1990s.

Panda Anderson, Alan Day, Machine gun Kelly the 'A' Team, on holiday

As you read my story you will see I give a running commentary on my thoughts on many of the big debates that have raged over the decades I refer to, from capital punishment to the betrayal by the grass. These are my pearls of wisdom, my overview on the psychology of crime and an insight, gained from years of real experience, into the mindset of a real villain.

One story I tell you relates to one man whose life was always inextricably linked to mine through the strongest bond imaginable and who I had not met for almost 70 years. His story proves, if proof is needed, that the experiences of childhood that shape the boy, later shape the man.

I consider myself retired now and I am suffering from ill health, due to slight brain damage, but my memory is as sharp as it has ever been.

In a sense this is not a crime book, that will follow this publication. This is a story in the main of the lives of two men. It is my true story.

My name is John 'Mario' Cunningham and, though I never gave myself the title, many in the know refer to me as the Geordie Godfather.

John 'Mario' Cunningham
July 2009

CHAPTER ONE

THE PRISON ESCAPE

THE SMELL was rancid, enough to make someone with a weak stomach, such as a screw, wretch and vomit. As dusk fell over Durham Prison I knew that if all went to plan I would soon be on my toes. My biggest risk was not so much getting out of what was considered to be one of the toughest jails in Britain but getting out of Durham City itself.

I had been filling the slop bin with rotten food for a couple of days and the smell from the pig swill permeated the air around the officers' mess where I had cunningly secured myself a job. The mess building was next door to the main gates, surrounded by secure large steel doors, barred windows and alarm bells. Although near the main gates, this area was very much inside the jail.

All I needed to do now was add a specially prepared concoction of chemicals into the bin which, when mixed with the slops, would make the stink unbearable.

What stood between me and freedom was one large steel door and that door would only need to be opened for just a few seconds whilst the duty screw's attention was distracted and I would be away.

My planning, as ever, had been meticulous and, of necessity, secretive. I had gained the confidence of another prisoner who I felt I could trust he would engage the screw in conversation at the precise moment I gave him the nod. I had lined up two working girls on the outside to meet me at a specific spot on the prison wall with clothes for me to change into. I knew the girls well and, like the fellow prisoner I had taken into my confidence, I knew they were not the type to betray me.

I knew my bid for freedom was audacious because in December, 1964, security at Durham Jail was the tightest it had ever been. Some of the UK's top villains were incarcerated in Durham, among them one of the Great Train Robbers, who had only recently been taken in as a new inmate from a jail in London, and infamous child killers such as John Straffen. What with another train robber, Ronnie Biggs, having recently escaped from another jail down south, Durham was on special high alert.

Mario in Durham

It was time to make my move. I gave my fellow inmate the nod and walked into the yard with a bucket full of the chemicals I had acquired, slowly lifted the swill bin lid, and poured the liquid over the rotten, maggot-infested leftovers. The reaction was, in a smelling sense, explosive and immediate. My fellow inmate talked to the screw who was bent double, clutching his guts and coughing and spluttering, about to be violently sick.

"We'll have to get the bin outside! It's stinking the fucking place out," I shouted. "Open the door and I'll shove it outside."

The prison officer puked and wiped his mouth with a handkerchief.

"Are you all right?" My mate, who was a good talker, asked him, as the screw took hold of his large key as he wretched in pain and opened the big steel door.

"Get the bloody thing out!" He pleaded.

Within seconds I dropped the bin, darted around and out of the main gate and legged it along the outside wall of the prison where, just as had been planned, my two women friends were waiting with a bag of clothes. We were only about 50 yards from the Durham City police headquarters in Old Elvet. We all ran a few more yards and came upon a smaller wall which I leapt over and then dragged my two friends with me as they were struggling.

Sitting on a grassed area by the wall my two friends were shaking and giggling, probably with the adrenaline rush and the thrill of the escape. They passed the clothes to me.

My prison-issue blue and white striped shirt came off my back within seconds and one of the lasses put it into her bag. I rolled my dark grey prison trousers up to above my knees. The blouse I was handed was a bit tight but suitably feminine, the stockings I just tucked into my rolled up trouser legs and, thankfully, the girls had got me a pair of flat shoes, not a manly-looking pair, more non descript. With the heavy, knee-length coat, buttons on the left, to keep out the bitter winter winds, and a patterned headscarf my transformation was almost complete. The lasses, both pretty girls, applied a little powder puff and lipstick but I drew the line at mascara! I mean, what does a man have to do?

As we walked into the bustling Durham City, with one of the lasses and me arms linked, most of the shops were closing for the day and workers were returning home. Within minutes the city centre was choked with police cars and vans, with sirens blaring and lights flashing, uniformed police dog handlers were all over the place, their Alsatians straining at the leash, and all roads into and out of the city had been cordoned off. Bizzies were everywhere, on the streets, in the shops, on the buses. All cars were being stopped and officers searched every boot. People were told to get out of their vehicles while they were searched and the fumes from exhaust pipes spewed into the cold night air creating a claustrophobic atmosphere. With all the noise, the flashing blue lights and the sirens blaring in the traffic snarl ups, the scene can only be described as chaos, absolute pandemonium.

We headed for the bus station in the city's North Road. I wasn't worried or anxious, I felt pretty cool about the whole thing. In the bus station café news of my escape had already hit the airwaves; it was the lead item on the local radio news. "An escaped prisoner is being hunted by police,"

[From the Chronicle and Journal December 1964]

Newcastle Man Breaks Jail

Police with dogs were out last night hunting an escaped prisoner from Durham Prison

They stopped and questioned drivers of vehicles, including buses, on all roads leading from the city after 23-year-old John Andrew Cunningham, of Newcastle, had escaped from the prison only 50 yards from the city police headquarters in Old Elvet. His description was put out to neighboring forces and police kept a watch on his home in Crown Street, Elswick, Newcastle.

Cunningham, who escaped under cover of darkness, is serving a 12-month sentence imposed at Newcastle Sessions on October 9th. Cunningham, is described as 5 feet 11 inches tall, slim, and has a fresh complexion, dark brown hair, blue eyes and an oval face.

When Cunningham escaped he was wearing a dark grey battle dress jacket, dark grey trousers, a blue and white striped shirt and a navy blue tie. Cunningham was charged at Newcastle magistrates' court on September 24th, with breaking into the offices of Presco Ltd., Spital Tongues, on the previous night, two other men were charged jointly with him.

Cunningham's escape makes it the Prisons biggest break for freedom in its 102 years

Mario in Durham

the news presenter could be heard saying. Then he went on to describe the man police were looking for: "Wearing a dark grey battle dress jacket, dark grey trousers, a blue and white striped shirt and a navy blue tie." The news man ended the item saying it was the biggest break for freedom from Durham Jail in 102 years. As we sipped a cup of tea I looked over to my female companions and winked. The bizzies and everyone else were looking for a bloke dressed in prison issue uniform - not an ordinary-looking working-class 'woman' out with her two friends.

After finishing our tea we went into the main bus station and got on the first bus we found that could get us out of the enclosed city, it was a double decker destined for Ferryhill, a typical mining village a few miles south of Durham. We sat upstairs in the back seats. As the bus reached the outskirts of the city into a long line of traffic the inevitable happened, it was stopped and two young police constables boarded. "What's going on officer," an old woman asked. "There's a man escaped from the prison," the officer said, as he walked up the aisle of the top deck, glancing at everyone on each side. He said to her that the prisoner had just escaped from work in the jail, which was untrue. I had not been shrinking from my duties as I had removed the horrible, smelly bin and done my work before I left 'work' to get my bus. It was a little bit of excitement for the passengers in what would probably have otherwise been a dull, unexceptional, day. The young cop's eyes met mine for a second. I didn't flinch and he turned round to leave. But before he left he smiled and gave me a wink! He bloody winked at me! I was more than a little perturbed, as I didn't realise I could make a convincing 'woman', and an attractive one at that. My heart had been pounding but I was well rehearsed and kept my cool. The satisfaction I got out of watching that little copper walk back down the aisle of the bus is impossible to put into words. When he got to the bottom I heard him say 'all clear upstairs' and then slowly the bus pulled away.

The scare was over as quickly as it had begun and the bus, which was packed with passengers, was allowed through the police cordon. The lasses I was with gave out a huge sigh of relief and we made our way to Ferryhill. I had always been convinced of my escape plan. Fleeing in a fast car would only have seen me stopped at a checkpoint and returned back to serve out my sentence. Escaping by foot in my prison garb I would have stuck out like a sore thumb, only to be quickly recaptured. I knew that what I needed to do was to go with the flow, to mingle with ordinary people. The bizzies would never have dreamt I would take the bus ... dressed as a woman.

I had only been in Durham Jail for about eight weeks after a conviction for breaking into offices in Spital Tongues, Newcastle, and for attacking a member of the police force. It was unfair as I only broke his nose which just happened to be in the right place at the wrong time. I was gutted not because of the twelve months sentence but because I had some very important business lined up which I really needed and wanted to sort out. The bit of business? All I can say is that it was so important for me to sort out it was worth the risk of me having it on my toes with the threat of a lengthier prison sentence on my recapture. I couldn't spend any more time languishing at Her Majesty's Pleasure while this bit of business hung over my head.

Eventually the bus arrived into Ferryhill and we got off. It was still too early to start jumping up and down with joy, but I thought if we dropped into a local pub and had a little drink then that would pass off a few hours whilst all those cops were flying around looking for me. When we went into the pub we went into the quiet back room and sat down. It was a very cosy little place. I then decided that it would be a good idea to sit there for a few hours to let things calm down as Durham was still in chaos and all the roads were still blocked. The police were obviously still not aware that I had already slipped through their so called escape proof jail and city.

I laughed my head off later when I discovered that my sister Margaret and her husband Billy were sitting down to a meal when all of a sudden my face appeared on the television news.

A few hours later, after a few drinks in Ferryhill, I was safely back in Newcastle but couldn't return to my home in Crown Street, Elswick, as it was still under police observations and would be for some considerable time.

News of my escape from Durham Jail spread through the North East underworld like wildfire, all the top men were taking about it, which did much to boost my status within the underworld 'family'. Although my bid for freedom was probably one of the more unusual there had been other escapes from Britain's toughest prison and there would be more.

Only three years earlier, in 1961, safe blower Ronnie Heslop, nicknamed "rubber bones" and "Houdini", from Page Bank, County Durham, dug himself free from Durham Prison over a period of four days using a teaspoon and kitchen knife after removing a ventilation grill from the cell floor. He swam the River Wear twice during his getaway and was on the run for six weeks before he was recaptured. Ronnie, who was a serving soldier at the time, had been charged with stealing £262 from a lemonade factory in Spennymoor and for attempting to blow a safe at the Ministry of Labour in the same County Durham town. I had met Ronnie Heslop several times, both on the inside, when we were both doing time and on the outside, as we had similar working patterns, blowing safes.

Within a few days of my escape I got my very important business done and decided to go to Mosside in Manchester to keep a low profile. Mosside was, at that time, and still is, as far as I know, mainly inhabited by West Indians. It was a very rough, violent and dangerous place and in the short time I was there several murders took place. The top men in Mosside had seen me on television; they knew I was a staunch player and that I could be trusted, so I was accepted by them and shown some respect. In Mosside the West Indians had their own illegal clubs called Shabeens and I was the only white bloke who they would allow in there, this being their inner sanctum. I learned a great deal from these people, they were indeed like a family to me. However, I also knew that I could not stay in one place for a long time, as I was a wanted man and my mug shot was appearing on television nearly every week. So after about four months I decided to go to Liverpool, there was a business man who the firm in Mosside wanted hurting and I offered to do it because I was moving on and when you are on the run you need cash all the time. Without going into too much detail I was given intelligence on the target, and then, at the right time, I cut one of the target's ears off with an extremely long sharp razor. It was all over in seconds. I was then well paid and I immediately fled to Liverpool where I had a great time. The Beatles were just starting to become hugely popular, the Cavern Club was the place to be, I had a lot of cash, a flash car, good, fashionable clothes and the women I met were stunning and not shy at coming forward. It was the start of the swinging sixties and a great time to be young.

16

Whilst in Liverpool I got on really well with the top people in the Liverpool underworld, it now appeared as though someone was guiding me and for some strange reason, wherever I went I was always accepted by the local top guys. When I talk about the underworld I am talking about guys who were professionals in crime, who would stick together and look after each other. I learned a lot from them, and this was to serve me well in my future jobs and exploits. The contacts I made then were to remain with me for many years. Not only did I learn a lot from them I even put in for my driving test, which I passed first time around, it doesn't sound much but remember not only did I have to hide my identity, but I also had to be more vigilant and careful as a driver. I could

A 'homecoming' cake

not take the chance of having an accident and ending up in court, which might have been disastrous as I had a lot to do before I was caught.

Keeping one step ahead of the law I had to make sure that everything I did was planned to the absolute letter, this included where I would go even when I needed to do some simple everyday thing such as get a new shirt, or even buy day-to-day groceries. This daily planning became the norm to me, as such it was to serve me on my later jobs and exploits, planning became an automatic reaction to everything I was doing. Whilst I was in Liverpool I carried out a few lucrative jobs, not really worth mentioning here, but the money was good. All the guys were going for a weekend in Blackpool for a good booze up, so off I went to Blackpool with them. To say I loved Blackpool would be an understatement, it was great and I told the lads that I was going to stick around Blackpool for a while, and that I would catch up with them again sooner or later.

One of the pubs I used to frequent regularly in Blackpool was, if I can remember correctly, owned by Brian London. London was a heavyweight boxer who had during his career fought Mohammed Ali, although he lost, not surprising when you look at Mohammed Ali's career. Anyway one night in the pub I had good cause to thrash this bloke and boy did he get it, in fact I lost it completely with him and done him some serious damage. I was later to learn that this bloke had a reputation of being one of the real tough guys in Blackpool, so it didn't do my reputation any harm, in fact it increased it. After that episode everyone gave me a lot of respect there and I truly enjoyed staying in Blackpool. During this time I met up with this lovely young woman from Preston, and by this time I also had a really flash sports car, and indeed life was on the up.

My career as a villain had really only just begun but after a few years I would be at the top of my game. How I got there I will soon reveal but to understand who I am and what I am you'll need to know where it all started ... and it's not a pleasant story.

CHAPTER TWO

PARENTS FROM HELL

THE WOMAN sat in total silence and in solitude on a hard, simply-made wooden chair, looking up at a high, but very small barred window, which only allowed a limited amount of daylight to enter and reflect into the cell in which she was trapped. The narrow shafts of sunlight that cut into the heavy darkness in the room served only to highlight the tiny, but many, speckles of dust that hung in the air, reminding the woman that, with every breath she took, her lungs would fill with the muck that engulfed her.

The woman looked around, her tired eyes resting on a low bed with a hard thin mattress and one threadbare blanket to keep out the cold. In the corner stood a chamber pot and on the top of a small, rough table in front of her lay a worn bible that had seen better days.

The daylight was beginning to fade and as semi-darkness fell a small gas lamp began to glow. The lamp was secured into a one foot square alcove situated near the thick steel door, which only opened when she was handed a battered steel plate containing a small amount of food which tasted repulsive and was almost inedible. The woman was thin and unhealthy looking. Her face was grey and gaunt and her eyes sunken. Within the skin of her face there were thin, red, thread veins, evidence of too much alcohol and not enough healthy food. The solitary woman, in a single cell for her own protection, had seen things in life she should never have seen and had done things she should have regretted, but her abnormal mind would not allow such thoughts to enter her addled brain. The woman was only 23. She was my mother.

In another part of the same prison and incarcerated under the same conditions was another prisoner also confined to solitary confinement. He was my father, then aged 26.

I was, at this time, in a children's home and I was only four months old, having been placed there by order of a court as being a seriously neglected child.

My mother Eilleen Cunningham and my father Peter had lived in small, dilapidated house in Peases Street, South Church, Bishop Auckland, a mining town in the heart of County Durham which, like many other towns and cities at the outbreak of World War II, was in the depths of a depression, with little food available for people who could ill afford it anyway. For those not yet signed up to fight there was a climate of uncertainty and fear.

As well as coal, minerals, limestone and ironstone were all mined in and around the area and transported through Bishop Auckland towards the coast and the town was an important centre in terms of the railways. The Shildon wagon works nearby employed many people and Darlington and Stockton, a few miles to the south and south west, were considered the birthplace of the railways. Before the outbreak of World War II there was employment in the town but with the rationing books, the blackout, the ever-present threat of enemy raids, and other restrictions placed on townsfolk, the early 1940s were bleak and depressing times.

Nevertheless, it seemed families, on the whole, stuck together and supported each other through the hard times, making sure children were clothed and fed as best as they could be. Indeed, it seemed that the misery of war and poverty strengthened the family bond.

Not so in the Cunningham household, where the conditions were so appalling that an inspector with the National Society for the Prevention of Cruelty to Children (NSPCC) told a court that the house was not fit for a dog to live in, never mind children.

My parents had been under observation by the NSPCC for some time, but nothing had improved their parenting skills. In 1940 an older boy (apparently my brother) had been shipped out to a children's home run by the Barnardo's charity and a baby girl (my sister) was so malnourished and ill-treated she died on admission to the Bishop Auckland Poor Law Institution. There had been talk of prosecuting my parents then, but they never appeared before magistrates at that time.

The authorities decided they had to do something, however, after a police officer visited our house and found me in a pram surrounded by blacking tins, empty tins, which I was lying on, and an empty bottle. I had been abandoned by both of my parents and my mother had not seen me for more than 24 hours. At the time my father had been living on 35 shillings a week unemployment assistance and my grandmother on my father's side lived nearby, but she didn't want to know me either.

Both my parents were given six months prison with hard

labour by magistrates in Bishop Auckland who described the case as "disgraceful". The case was duly reported in the Auckland Chronicle. Where most parents would have hanged their heads in shame at their appalling cruelty and filthy living conditions becoming public knowledge, it would not have bothered by mother and father one iota.

And so it was that a sister of mine who I would never see was dead, a brother of mine I would probably never see had been shipped off to a children's home and both my parents were in jail because of their neglect of me, a babe in arms only four months old.

How could this have happened, even in the early 1940s? And how could it have been allowed to happen? I was just one small boy, neglected, unfed and uncared for but there were many thousands of other boys and girls just like me up and down the country, all let down by the very authorities put in place to protect them. This was gross neglect on a huge scale and it was those at the sharp end of the neglect and cruelty, the children, whose lives were destined to be lived out in a world which they would understandably view as uncaring and even hostile.

These children, like me, it appeared, never had a chance.

* *

Harry S with other Barnardo's kids.

Harry S felt as though he had been travelling for days though, in truth, he had been on the road for about six hours after a very early start, being shouted from his bed as the cock crew on a patch of land near the home in Falkirk, Scotland. He was leaving behind him other children that he knew; children that he had played with in the schoolyard. Most of the youngsters had broad Scottish accents and often Harry S couldn't understand a word they were saying, particularly the youngsters from Glasgow who even seemed to talk differently to the other Scottish children. As the car he was in headed for Fincham in Norfolk, Harry couldn't remember much about the home he had just left, other than being showered down with a hosepipe with other boys of his age, all standing in a line with their hands on their private parts. There had been lessons, in English, Maths and Arithmetic, colouring books, porridge oats for breakfast, the strong smell of cabbage at lunchtime and the early-to-bed nights, more tolerable in the winter than in the summer when he and the other children just wanted to go outside. The only other thing that stuck in his mind was the permanent smell of carbolic soap.

As the car turned into Fincham village the man driving said: "You'll like it here, Harry. There's other children your age and plenty to see and do." He smiled and Harry just looked at him.

The house was large, detached, and set back from the road with its own drive. Harry S thought it must have many bedrooms. It looked like a house he had seen in a book. As he stood on the large front step alongside his mentor, his bag by his side, the door opened and a stout woman in her 50s with bright red hair and a matronly look glanced at Harry's face and smiled.

"This is Mrs Harvey," the man said. "She is your new foster mother."

"Hello Harry," said Mrs Harvey. "You come inside and we'll get you something to eat and a nice drink of lemonade. You've had a long, long journey."

Harry's mentor said his goodbyes and Mrs Harvey led him into the dining room of the house, which had a large, round table, covered in a pristine white tablecloth, at which sat a boy about a year or so younger than Harry and a girl about his own age.

"This is Harry," said Mrs Harvey. "He has come to us all the way from bonny Scotland. Sit yourself down lad." She turned her attention to the other two children. "This is Peter," she said. "And this pretty little girl is his sister, Janet."

Peter and Janet were sitting at the table eating a sandwich and drinking orange juice. Mrs Harvey put a plate down in front of Harry with a sandwich as big as a doorstop, so he started munching away and sipping his glass of lemonade. Peter and Janet just stared at him, initially not saying a word.

After she finished her meal Janet asked: "Where's your mum and dad?"

"I don't know," said Harry.

"Do you have a mum and dad?" Asked Peter.

"I don't know," said Harry.

"You don't know much, do you?" Said Janet, at which she and Peter started giggling. Harry just sat and continued eating his sandwich.

The village of Fincham, in the heart of Norfolk and surrounded by undulating fields, left much for Harry and his new found friends to explore. With the working Bircham Windmill nearby, the Fenlands on the doorstep, the splendid church of St Martin's, the Tudor Manor House of Fincham Hall and King's Lynn only 12 miles north, Harry had found himself in a quintessentially English country village, so different for him to what had gone before.

He spent his first night in his new home in a comfortable bed and slept like a log.

CHAPTER THREE

INTO THE ORPHANAGE

As a long line of boys stood to attention, almost military style, in the large hall, the big doors swung open loudly and two nuns dragged a 12-year-old boy by his arms, along the polished floor like a rag doll, as he kicked and screamed to be set free. Other nuns stood looking on, along with some masters ready to move in and help out if the boy became too difficult to handle. The rest of the boys, like me, just stood there in silence, watching as our fellow housemate protested his innocence, but his cries just fell on deaf ears. It appeared the boy had run away the previous day, ending up in Barnard Castle, County Durham, where some local person thought he looked out of place and informed the police. The police duly brought him back to where he should have been.

One of the nuns pushed the boy over a table, bent double, and called for two other boys standing in line, to hold each of his arms down whilst a fellow nun kept hold of his legs. The boy struggled and screamed but the more he did so, the more angry the nuns appeared to be and the more forceful in pinning him down. When suitably restrained one of the nuns then pulled down the boy's trousers and pants, exposing his white backside for all to see. In normal circumstances you might have expected the boys witnessing this event to giggle, either in shock or embarrassment, but these were not normal circumstances and all the boys just stood looking on. Most had witnessed before what I was about to see for the first time.

As the nuns and their two young accomplices held the boy down, one of the masters stepped forward with his weapon of punishment, not a single cane but several canes tied together for the sole purpose of causing as much pain and damage as possible. This was my first sight of the birch, and it would not be my last.

With a look of sadistic pleasure in his eyes the master brought the birch down hard on the boy's bare backside and the cracking sound reverberated around the hall, followed in quick succession by a piercing, shrill, scream, from the boy, who screwed his face in agony and clenched his fists knowing there was more to come. The strokes came quickly; a three-second pause, the master lifts his right hand as far as he can, and then, crack, the canes strike. For the boys who had witnessed such beatings in the past, and those who had been on the receiving end, they looked on and their faces hardly flinched. For the boys who were witnessing this sadism for the fist time, their eyes were wide and faces white with shock. Some of the younger boys were crying but not allowing their cries to be audible, fearing they would be next for the birch.

This was life in St Mary's Orphanage in Tudhoe, County

Durham, where I was placed by the Roman Catholic "care" system from the age of four. There were scores of other boys placed in the same orphanage, many from County Durham but more from Tyneside, some genuinely orphaned in tragic circumstances, but most, like me, neglected and abandoned by their parents.

The brutality we all witnessed in that home was something none of us children should have been forced to witness. The beatings were regular, if not with the birch then sometimes

Brother Michael

with a cricket bat, and the nuns and masters ruled by fear. This was not a place of "caring" for the less fortunate in the community, this was a place of pure evil where some of the staff took real pleasure in inflicting pain on innocent children and putting them through real psychological torture.

I remember when I was about four or five when a nun called me to her. She was holding a small child in her arms and she said 'Do you know who this is?' On getting no physical or emotional response

Sister Margaret

she simply said 'This is your brother Michael'. Some years later I was also introduced to a young girl who I was told was my sister Margaret.

After only seeing Margaret briefly she was then sent away somewhere else and I never saw her again for many years. I found out later that, yet again, my mother and father had been sent to prison for seriously neglecting my sister and brother, Margaret and Michael, so my parents were back in prison for a second time. They had obviously learned nothing.

Although Michael and I ended up as children in the same strict Catholic Orphanage, as I was older, Michael was in a different section – the junior's section – and I did not get to see him much. In fact the staff were happy to keep us apart. Life in St Mary's Orphanage and home in Tudhoe Village was nothing less than horrible. There was regular corporal punishment, floggings meted out to the boys and, more often than not, these were carried out in public in front of the other 'inmates'. This place was run by what was nothing less than fear and I was there for many years. During the many terrible years that I was there I was never shown any kind of love nor even anything like basic affection; we were never cuddled, never kissed, all we had during these years was the constant brutality and the never ending screams of floggings.

This place was absolutely dreaded by all that were trapped in it, bad things happen in life but not every day, some were given floggings for trying to run away, some had to sit in freezing baths until the staff thought that this punishment had served it's purpose, some had to kneel for hours on the cold stone floors reciting prayers until the staff again thought that the punishment had been fully served. Other punishments were regularly used here and the screams from the youngsters have lived with me all my life. I swear I can still hear them sometimes when I go to sleep, even after all these years. I can still hear the screams and see the tears of kids shouting out for a mother or father, crying for them to intervene, pleading to get them to stop the beatings that they were being forced to endure, but their pleas were never heard and were always ignored by most of the staff in that terrible place.

As a result of this treatment many boys wet the bed, however as soon as this was discovered the bed wetter would be dragged to the bath area then thrown into the freezing bath, again scream-ing with cold and fear. Some children were actually seriously injured in this process, but they had their own doctor in the orphanage and they simply told him that there had been an acci-dent. This doctor would then simply accept this untrue tale and this was always accepted without question. We had no one to turn to or to plead with for help against these sadistic people who, in effect, owned us, lock, stock and barrel.

By sending me to St Mary's Orphanage in Tudhoe Village, all things considered, the authorities didn't send me anywhere to be protected, did they? In fact what was more cruel? What my mother and father had done to me in my early months, or what the Court did by sending me to this place to live in constant fear and having to endure the terrible conditions that I was forced to endure for so many miserable years?

We as children had nobody to turn to and I can remember the constant crying at night of other young children crying for their families, even those that had been previously treated badly in the past by their parents, they still cried, they cried out for them for months and sometimes for years.

Some of the staff in this place were nothing less than sadistic and carried out their duties with what can only be called pre-meditated brutality, this is what I had to endure for the whole of my early childhood. Try to imagine the suffering and humiliation that goes with this early part of my life. Not one member of the staff of that orphanage was ever charged or convicted for their atrocious behaviour towards the children placed in their care. There was no way out of this living Hell, we were constantly frightened, had nobody to turn to, so is it any wonder that I have grown up with a deep mistrust of authority?

As you know, we were stuck in this Hell whilst many were stuck in another Hell, they were fighting the War in Europe, and we were constantly reminded of this, that they were there dying for us, to make things better, well it was falling on deaf ears, nothing got better, it seemed only to go from bad to worse. The food that we were given was disgraceful, for many years after I would look at simple things like a slice of bread and wonder why it didn't have any green bits in it, let alone knowing that you could actually fold it without it breaking into a million pieces.

* *

The village primary school in Fincham, Norfolk, only had about a dozen pupils in each class, which was probably to be expected when considering the village population was only a few hundred.

Each of the pupils had their own desks with their own ink wells and there was a formal atmosphere to the school, discipline was maintained but there was no real need for corporal punishment as, generally, all the pupils were well behaved and showed respect for their teachers and each other.

Young Harry S had settled in well with his new foster parents and the other two children who stayed with him, brother and sister Janet and Peter, who also attended the same village school, Janet in the same class as Harry as they were both the same age.

The days were spent mainly on reading, writing and arithmetic and Harry S had an average aptitude towards those subjects but what he really excelled at was geography. He loved looking at the beautiful photographs in the many books he read showing exotic locations in faraway lands and dreamed that, perhaps, one day he would travel the world.

His time at the Barnardo's Children's Home in Scotland was now a distant memory and Harry was enjoying his time living in Fincham and attending the local school. As far as he was aware there was only himself and Janet and Peter attending the school who were foster children, but the three were never singled out for bullying or special treatment; they were all just young boys and girls growing up together.

Harry S had made friends with quite a few of the village boys and they would get up to mischief, as any boy would, stealing apples from the local orchard or turnips from the local farmer's field. He and his friends would all meet up on a Saturday to walk to the local picture house for the Saturday morning movies and escape for a couple of hours into the make-believe world of cowboys and indians or space travel. A few pennies from his foster mother for sweets thrown in, Harry enjoyed his time at the week-end picture house. A few of his friends thought Harry a bit of an oddity at first, with his strange Northern accent which several thought was Scottish. They knew he wasn't a violent boy or a bully, but there was something about Harry S that convinced them he could handle himself. They all thought he was a bit of a tough lad but knew he wouldn't harm anyone unless he was defending himself. There might have been a few boyish arguments, but none of the young Fincham lads were going to pick a fight with Harry.

Home life for Harry S was pretty relaxed but his foster mother Mrs Harvey did have certain standards to maintain, particularly when it came to cleanliness, of the mind and body, and tidiness within the house. So Harry S would help out, keeping his room tidy and even helping Mrs Harvey clean the house when he could. And he made sure he always polished his shoes and took regular baths.

He would walk to and from school with Janet and Peter, play games with them in the house and Mrs Harvey would often take them on day trips to special attractions in and around the county. Harry S had grown so attached to Janet and Peter that he regarded them as his own brother and sister.

He didn't know who he was, or where he was from, and he didn't think about it and he never asked. As a young boy, about to enter his teenage years, Harry S was happy.

CHAPTER FOUR

NUMBER NINE

"Do you reject Satan?"

"We reject Satan!"

"Do you reject Satan?"

"We reject Satan!"

It was the same every day, sometimes at different times of the day, but all we St Mary's orphan boys would have to sit there clutching our Catechisms and reciting the words so often they would be engrained in our minds, ready to speak out loudly whenever the nuns or masters asked us the questions. If we didn't say the words with conviction, as if we really meant them, then we'd get a slap over the face or be told to leave the room and come back for a beating with the birch.

The Catechism was bad enough, but there was also compulsory and regular attendance at mass, which would go on for a couple of hours, the priest reciting everything in Latin, to which we were expected to respond in Latin, and some of the boys would be on the altar in their pristine red cassocks and white aprons, waving sweet-smelling incense. It was all so ritualistic and monotonous but perhaps those are the two key ingredients for effective indoctrination, rituals that never change and go back centuries and the repetition of words or phrases ad nauseum (that's a bit of Latin, too).

During the mass we would all be expected to take communion, the round piece of flat, unleavened bread, which was supposed to represent the body of Christ. We just had to stick our tongues out for the priest to place it there, and we weren't to chew on it, just let it dissolve in our mouths. If a boy didn't take communion then questions were asked. The only excuse was that you were a sinner and you needed to go to confession, to cleanse your soul and leave it pure enough to take communion. We were expected to go to confession every week, whether we had sinned or not. The nuns would tell us we were all sinners, that we must have sinned, and therefore have something to confess, and if we hadn't sinned then we must have at least thought about committing a sin, and that was a sin in itself. You just couldn't bloody win! Most of the boys ended up confessing to 'sins' which were nothing more than a figment of their own fertile imaginations. So we all went to confession every week, and we all took communion and for a moment, just a moment, the nuns and the masters were happy.

Every morning at the crack of dawn we would have to be up, dressed and ready, to go outside into the main courtyard, regardless of the weather, to kneel down on the hard concrete floor with our Rosary beads in our hands looking up to the huge statue of St Mary the Virgin, the saint blessed with the name of our orphanage. And then, in unison, came the repetition: "Hail Mary, full of grace... Hail Mary, full of grace... Hail Mary...". It was enough to drive a boy to distraction.

On a Sunday evening it was Benediction and we would walk the "stations of the cross", retracing Jesus's steps towards his crucifixion, reciting a prayer each time we stopped. Every evening before we got into bed we would be expected to kneel by our beds to thank God for everything we had and ask him to bless the nuns and masters who 'cared' for us and to forgive us for our sins (it's those sins again!). And while we waited for sleep to come a nun, in her long black robe and white headgear, would stand at the head of the dormitory stairs like a still ghost, staring at us boys below.

In the early morning it would be a cold shower before dressing and prostrating ourselves before the statue of the Virgin Mary for morning prayers. The showers were cold, very cold, and I grew up thinking that was actually how you took a shower, with cold bloody water! It was during these showers that the sexual predilections or perversions of some of the nuns and the masters would manifest themselves. The nuns and masters would stand there staring at our young, naked bodies, paying particular attention to our private parts. They would utter things like "make sure you wash your necks properly" and the like but their main preoccupation was staring at our pre-pubescent genitalia. Some of the staff, who were supposed to abstain from sex, were absolutely obsessed by it. If they caught a boy masturbating in bed, and at our young ages and the circumstances we found ourselves in a wank was a comfort and a pleasure, the boy would be dragged from his bed, kicking and screaming, to be flogged with the birch or a cane, usually with all the other boys forced to look on. It was as if some of the nuns and masters actually got a kick, some kind of sexual gratification, at seeing our naked bodies in the showers, then beating our bare arses with the birch if we ever laid so much as a finger on our cocks. They were all - well, some of them - fucking perverts.

Stripping us of any kind of dignity, beating us repeatedly, forcing us to recite prayers several times a day, forcing us to attend mass and to pray to the Virgin Mary every morning, forcing us to eat almost inedible food, forcing us to work like slaves and then depriving us of any kind of affection, from a longed-for cuddle to a warm, parental-like, embrace, should really have satisfied even the most sadistic thirsts of some of the staff. But no. To complete the dehumanising process they took from us the only thing we had left - our names. All the staff referred to us not by our names, but by numbers. I was number nine.

St Mary's Home for Boy's or Orphanage was actually once known as Tudhoe Home Certified Poor Law School for Girls, originally only taking in girls. It was not until 1939 that boys were also admitted. The Home admitted children for various reasons and they were not always orphans, some were quite simply abandoned and more or less left to rot in this place. One of my friends in this place was John Killeen, he was number eight. I sat down with John recently and asked him if he would like to make a list of what he remembered about this place, to be honest I already knew what it would be like, but it was also for another reason. Most of the lads that were incarcerated in this place have found it hard to deal with, and the after effects in some cases have left a mark on those that have not been able to release or talk about what happened to them.

Number nine (that's me) always seemed to be in trouble for one reason or another, but like numbers one to eight and numbers ten upwards, everyone had to endure the constant threat of something happening. If anyone did anything wrong, no matter how trivial, we would all have to stand up in the gym for anything between four and six hours. Some just couldn't handle this and fainted crashing to the floor, and would be left there. They made us stand there, worse still we couldn't do anything to help those that had collapsed, they made us stand there until the person in charge got fed up – we didn't matter one bit. One thing that I have lived with and that still sends a shiver through my body is the cold, freezing baths that we were thrown into. On one occasion I remember a lad being thrown in for wetting the bed. When they threw him into this bath he hit his head and was unconscious, they just pulled him by the hair out from under the water and left him there. I often think that if they had turned around and walked away he would have been a goner for sure, that spectacle has remained with me to this day. I remember complaining to a boy for making a noise when he got up during the night, they just dragged me from bed and threw me into the cold bath, they always kept it full of cold water waiting for a visitor, and it never had to wait long. The cold bath was well used; we were made to have a bath once a week, even though you may have been tossed into it during the week, over fifty of us had to bath in this and it was absolutely foul and stunk by the fiftieth one.

On the brighter side, with the Dracula-style looking building in which I spent my childhood being situated in the countryside, I remember spending long periods of time staring out an upstairs window during the summer and watching the sheep, cows and birds. I would look at the green grass and the flowers swaying in the breeze and I would see a farmer in the distance ploughing his field. My young mind would wonder why I could not be as free as the birds, as colourful as the flowers, I would look up at the bright blue sky, I would dream, dream and dream, then I would turn away from the window and look around the gloomy room and realise that it really was all a dream, it was never meant to be.

It may sound a bit corny or appear to be self pity, but being a child in that forbidding building really did make me realise that I really was nobody's child. It was a nightmare. I felt totally lost. I felt totally rejected and alone and worse, insecure. Just how could a mother, or anyone, cause a child to suffer so much? I would look at the other children and see the sadness and fear in their eyes, we would just look at each other, we were just too young to understand, too young to talk and discuss amongst ourselves what this was all about, we could not make any sense of it at all. We were emotionally wrecked, with no one to turn to, we had never known any type of kindness. How and why can it be that innocent children were put into this position, doomed to a childhood so cruel it would mean that we were scarred for life? The people responsible for causing so much suffering to children are not human, they are nothing less, in my eyes, than *evil beyond belief* – what is worse is that it could still be happening to this day in other *caring* institutions.

＊＊＊

THE water in the outdoor swimming pool at the Parkstone Sea Training School on the outskirts of Poole, Dorset, didn't look that inviting. Perhaps that was because it was February, 1950, and the temperature outside the water was only four or five degrees above freezing. As thirteen-year-old Harry S stood poolside with another six or so young cadets under the supervision of a naval officer he could feel the pimples rise on his skin and the thought of entering the water in the next few seconds filled him with much anxiety. It's not that he hadn't been in the water before; he'd enjoyed going to the local baths near Fincham in Norfolk with his friends Janet and Peter on outings with their foster mother, Mrs Harvey. The three of them would have great fun in the pool, Peter and Harry S "bombing" their young girl friend as she did the doggy-paddle in the shallow end, and then messing about under water, seeing how long they could hold their breaths. Janet could swim, well, in a fashion she could, with her feet not far from the bottom and her head always fully out of the water as her arms and legs gave her some motion. Peter could also keep himself afloat and swim a little, like Janet he had only mastered the doggy-paddle. Harry, on the other hand, had never swam, he had just bobbed up and down in the water, enjoying the company of his friends. As he now stood on the edge of the big swimming pool at the training school, facing the deep end, he wished he had at least attempted to swim, even with a floater in his hands and those inflatable arm bands worn by novices on his arms. At least he would have had an idea.

"All right, you lot!" Shouted the supervisor, looking at the scrawny, bony, bodies in front of him.

"You can't take to the sea, if you can't take to the water."

"Now, eyes closed, take a deep breath, and wait for my cue."

Harry stood shivering, holding his breath hard and wanting to breathe out, as he waited for the supervisor's next move, a wait which seemed to last a lot longer than it probably did.

Then he felt it, a heavy push on his back, and he was falling like a dead weight.

"You'll sink or you'll bloody well swim!" The supervisor shouted, as he went along the line of boys, pushing each one into the deep end.

Harry felt his feet touch the bottom and panic set in. He lunged his arms at the water, as if he was trying to hit his way out from inside a large paper bag, and he kicked his feet rapidly. He had to open his mouth, he couldn't hold it much longer, and he gulped as chlorine-filled dirty water entered his stomach and he coughed and he spluttered. As he floated to the top, his arms and legs flailing, his head bobbed out of the water and he spotted the supervisor looking on, shouting something which, to him, sounded like a series of dull thuds. Harry went down for a second time and he could feel his heart racing. He tried to hold his breath and he tried to focus. What did Janet do? He thought. How did she move in the water? Feeling nauseous now, as if he was about to vomit any minute, Harry again surfaced and everything he saw was blurred, even the bright sun above. He was about to go down for the third time.

"Move your fucking arms and move your fucking legs!" Shouted the supervisor, staring down at Harry from the pool side.

Harry tilted his body to the left, then moved his right arm and leg through the water, then tilted to the right and did the same, and suddenly he wasn't sinking any more. He was swimming. As he paddled his hands and arms through the water, he kept his head above it, and moved as quickly as he could to the pool side and the steps. He wanted to get out quickly.

Harry climbed the metal steps, stood at the side, and coughed and spluttered. He wanted to get rid of the water he had swallowed.

The supervisor handed him a towel. "Welcome to the Navy, son," he said. "You've got your water legs, now all you need is your sea legs!" The supervisor slapped Harry S on the back, in a friendly, father-like gesture, and Harry, for the first time in his life, felt good about himself, as if he had finally achieved something.

The 250-mile journey from Fincham to the training school had been a long and tiring one by bus and by train. Leaving Mrs Harvey and Janet and Peter, as they stood at the station waving him off, had been a bit of a wrench for Harry S and he felt his Adam's apple harden and his eyes glisten over. But he didn't want to cry. He wanted to show the only mum and brother and sister he knew, or at least he looked upon them as such, that he was no longer a vulnerable Barnardo's boy in need of care and attention. He was growing up, fast, and embarking on an adventure which just might see him fulfill the dreams he had had at the village school in Fincham all those years ago whilst studying geography; the dream of travelling to foreign, exotic, far-off lands. Harry knew he was to see the world.

The Parkstone Sea Training School, which was run by the Barnardo's charity, aimed to train young people, mainly those from disadvantaged backgrounds like Harry, for a future career in the Merchant Navy or the Royal Navy. Hundreds of young boys had trained at Parkstone over the years, most when it was the Russell Cotes Nautical School and the Watts Naval Training School. When Harry had arrived in 1950 the school had only just been amalgamated and given the name Parkstone. All the boys were issued with the standard sailor suits or "Number Ones" and with jerseys and flannels and shorts as working clothes. The staff of nautical instructors, captains and other trainers, were tough on discipline, but not harsh, and though boys could expect corporal punishment for misdemeanours, it was not a brutal regime that Harry found himself in.

Harry S Merchant Navy Cadet

The centre was vast, covering 34 acres, one mile north east of Poole and three-and-a-half miles west of Bournemouth. It had a great history, turning out trained seamen, many of whom had fought in the Second World War with great distinction. In 1940 sailors from the centre had witnessed much action at Poole, when the Battle of Britain was raging, witnessing dog fights and aircraft being shot out of the sky. Poole Harbour had been a base for civilian Sunderland flying boats and the Germans used to follow them in and machine-gun them when they landed.

At any one time up to 300 boys would be training at Parkstone, accommodated in dormitories in one of five "houses"; Howard House, Johnston House, Arranmore House, Broughton House and Jellicoe Hall, each named after the centre's generous benefactors.

The boys would be trained in all things nautical, from tying knots to cleaning and using rifles, and would stay for three to five years, depending on their age on arrival, before leaving for the Merchant Navy or Royal Navy and the distant shores of the world. On the centre's estate, as well as the dormitories, there were workshops, a chapel, dining hall and kitchen, an isolation block, accommodation for the staff and superintendents, as well as a grand central building known as Lady Russell-Cotes House, again named after a wealthy and charitable benefactor.

With views over Poole Harbour and the sea, Harry was happy at the centre and on a clear day he could see his destiny. There was a great camaraderie among all the boys and Harry made some great young friends. Every morning they would be marked off for breakfast in the dining hall, always porridge and so thick and hard the boys nicknamed it "Rock of Gibraltar". All had to eat it, and if any body refused he would feel a sharp pain on the head from the ladle used by one of the staff to dish the revolting porridge out.

Saturdays were free time for all the boys and Harry and his friends would generally visit a local picture house they knew as "The Big Hutch Cinema" because it looked like a big hutch and they would enjoy a plate of chips on the afternoon. On Sundays many of the boys would nip down to Poole Harbour, which was meant to be out of bounds, and get themselves on to the coal boats or the cobles, messing about on the water. It was at this time Harry took up what was to become a lifelong habit, smoking cigarettes. His cigarettes of choice in those days, like for many sailors, was Senior Service, very strong cigarettes which took a while to get used to.

As well as the training there were many other activities at the centre the boys could sign up for. Harry joined a rope-climbing display team and enjoyed showing off his climbing skills. He also learned to play the cornet under the tutelage of bandmaster Bandy Joyce, though he could never figure out if Bandy was his real name or his nickname. Harry could have joined the choir, but decided against it.

Harry would be spending the next three years of his life at Parkstone Sea Training School. He had learned to swim, been trained in weaponry and all things nautical and made some great friends. There was one thing he sensed above all else with the scores of boys with whom he shared his training and his dormitory – he felt that he belonged.

CHAPTER FIVE

THE RED JUMPER

AS I sat on a wooden chair, my arms held by two nuns, another nun cut into my hair with a pair of semi-sharpened scissors which left blood pouring down my face and neck. My hair was being pulled out in clumps because the scissors didn't work properly, but the nuns didn't care about that, they could see I was in pain and shouting in agony and this probably gave them some pleasure. Other boys in the home were forced to stand and watch.

After the ordeal of having my head shorn, which left small stumps of hair and big patches of baldness, I was ordered to put on a red jumper and wear it every day for several days. This jumper singled me out as having done something terrible, committing a sin, and it sent a stern message to the rest of the boys that they would get the same treatment if they did something to break the strict rules of the place.

My sin or crime was simply to run away. There had been nothing unusual happening in the home, I was just sick of the constant beatings and floggings and other physical and mental torture meted out to us boys. I didn't know where I was headed, I didn't even know which direction was north and south, I just knew I had to get away from that place.

One morning after a breakfast of stale porridge I waited for the coast to clear and legged it out of the front door, running as fast as my little legs could carry me. It was a cold morning and there was frost on the ground, but I ran as fast as I could, putting as much distance between me and the home as possible. I thought about where I could go and then a small fact hit me – I didn't have a home to run to, no parents, no relations, not even an aunt or uncle I could turn to in my hour of need. I just kept walking, then running, and eventually as I walked across a farmer's field I was met by two police officers, bundled into their van, and taken straight back to the home. It appeared someone in a village I had passed through recognised me as a St Mary's boy and contacted the authorities. It was a regular thing for boys to try to escape from the home, and the punishment they received when they were

38

inevitably caught was always the same, the hair cut and torn from their heads, a cold bath, and then the issue of the red jumper to mark them out, like the Jews were marked out for persecution during the war with their little yellow stars.

I was only twelve years old when I finally snapped and tried to run away, resulting in the severe punishment. I cannot remember what was going through my mind when I did this, I just snapped like a twig. Many years later a psychologist told me that I was extremely seriously and emotionally damaged. This was mainly due to never being shown any kind of love, nor even a cuddle or kiss that we all know now are very important in the development of any child. I am now over 60 years old and I am still unable to show any emotion. I feel that my children must have wondered why I was so remote and so very different to other fathers, and regret the upbringing that I had to endure in St Mary's Orphanage for having made me like this.

Bearing in mind that no child in the eleven years that I was incarcerated there in St Mary's Home escaped serious abuse of one kind or another, if it was not your turn to be the victim of a flogging, you and all the other children were forced to watch and sometimes forced to take part in the abuse, by having to hold the victim of the beating down across two tables.

At St Mary's Orphanage there was only at the very most four staff in charge of each section, nursery, juniors and seniors, other people working there were a couple of people working in the kitchen and laundry and I remember there was a gardener called Mr. Donnelly, we did not have any real contact with these people.

One day we were ordered by the Nuns to go to a room, were we were surprised to find some toys laid out for our 'pleasure', well that's what they wanted, they ordered us to be on our best behaviour as a photographer was going to take our picture. They obviously wanted to portray this awful place as a little part of heaven to those in the outside world. What a joke, the photograph later published in the newspaper showed on everyone's face the misery we had to endure.

We had regular bed inspections in the home. One strict rule was that we all had to sleep with our arms on top of the blankets. In my naivety, like most of the other boys, I didn't at first realise why this rule was in place. Throughout the night we would be checked on by the nuns, and if our hands were under the blanket, we would be dragged out of bed and forced into saying ten Hail Mary's, begging the Virgin Mary for forgiveness. I learned later when I started getting an erection what this was all about; we were so brain washed with all this Hell stuff, we would be afraid to touch ourselves, which is a natural part of growing up, for the fear of damnation, being struck down on the spot, and burning in Hell. The beatings and other abuse was bad enough but we boys did not want to burn in Hell. With the daily prayers, mass, the rules and the fear the masters and nuns instilled in us, we boys honestly believed we were destined for eternal damnation if we stepped out of line.

Saturday's were meant to be special, and they were, but only for the very few. Saturday's were visitors' day, but for many of us this just piled on the misery, as we didn't have any visitors. The nuns, who called themselves the Sisters of Charity, knew this, but it didn't stop them from singling some of us out to stand like two little guards at the front door to welcome the visitors. We would sit there and wait, hoping expectantly that someone would come to visit us, someone that we could greet and talk to, but it never happened. They were always there for somebody else and as every Saturday came and passed there was scores of boys who never received one visitor.

Young people, especially in the environment in which we grew up, are naturally inquisitive, but us boys would often regret asking the staff questions. One of the boys asked a nun if she had any hair under her stiff headgear. The little sinner's curiosity was met with a severe beating. We were told nothing and we learned not to ask any questions. If we were late for school the teachers broke into a weird smile, which said it all. We got the inevitable caning from the teacher, but the double whammy on this indiscretion was that they then told the nuns, who would give us another caning to make sure that we had learned a lesson. We quickly learned that being the last one back from school was not a good thing either, as the last one home had to clean and polish all the shoes of the other boys, not a nice job with the mud on them during the winter. We were in effect being trained and groomed for the army, if we didn't say "Sir" and say it with conviction, then it was off to be caned once more, it just went on and on. The cane was bad, but the birch left you in no doubt.

The most important thing that I can see now is that the abusers were mainly the people in charge of a section, which only amounts to a dozen people and a so called Sister Superior, every one of them were nothing less than serial abusers. In fact it was just a way of life to them: St Mary's Orphanage or home was indeed an abusers' paradise. There was no one and nothing at all to stop or deter them. We children had no protection whatsoever. I now reflect on this and realize that it was a horrific nightmare, and what disturbs me more is that I would find it very hard to believe that going by the law of averages, and the untold number of vicious physical attacks on children, I fear that the abusers must have over the years gone over the top with the abuse which may have resulted in the death of children there in that home.

Compared to other children's fathers, this being one of the reasons I am writing this book, I want my children to try and understand why their dad was unlike all of the other dads. I was once told by two women friends who did not know each other that I was incapable of showing emotion or love and in fact one of them said that I had a heart of pure stone. What was worse was that they were quite probably right as I have had many relationships, none of which worked out. I have been on my own now for over twenty years and I do get lonely at times, but I also realise that for me that it couldn't have been any other way.

* *

THE gale force winds and mountainous seas meant the decks were constantly awash with hundreds of tons of water and all five feet two of Harry S's frame was taking the brunt of the spray as he made his journey along the flying bridge clasping a message he needed to take to one of the officers. On the leeward side of the bridge housing he watched the bow lunge in and out of the waves as walls of water came crashing over the windlass. With several trips like this every four hours, then eight hours off for sleeping, Harry was gaining his sea legs in the same way that he had learned how to swim, by being thrown into the deep end. His frame was wrapped in a huge, new, oilskin coat which was as stiff as a board, but it kept the rain out and Harry S didn't care how ridiculous he looked. As a bridge boy on his first ship he was at the bottom rung of the ladder, last in the pecking order, so he would tolerate the verbal abuse from some of the officers who should have known better, and the constant toing and froing from one side of the ship to the other, delivering hand-written messages and then, as a deck boy, delivering plates of food to the officers' mess. The sailor's would often refer to him as their 'peggy' and at first he thought this a derogatory term, but later he discovered all bridge boys and deck boys were referred to by the same word. The combined din of the atrocious weather and the continual throb of the ship's engines below the galley were ever present, making it difficult for Harry to get any sleep in between his shifts around the clock, but he was getting used to it.

At the age of 15, having left Parkstone Sea Training School near Poole, Harry had made the short trip along the south coast to Southampton, Harry had signed up for his first sea voyage with the Merchant Navy aboard the Edinburgh Castle, a 28,000-ton vessel built in 1948 at the Belfast yards of Harland and Wolf and launched on its first journey by Princess Margaret.

When Harry had first sight of his first ship anchored at Southampton and about to set sail for South Africa he wondered in boyish amazement at the size of the vessel, which was 747ft long, the mechanisms that made it all work, and the huge number of people on board. He wondered how the hell it could stay afloat. The ship had departed Southampton on a Thursday afternoon at 4pm on a cold December day and Harry was excited. This was his first time off dry land and the ship was to call at Las Palmas in the Med followed by a ten-day sprint to Cape Town, then on to Port Elizabeth before arriving in Durban. This is what Harry had signed up for; to see some of the world, and his time on shore, seeing the sights and meeting new, and interesting, people made up for all the hassle on board of running here and there like a little gofer for the powers that be.

One thing Harry seemed to get covered in when on deck was rust. Apparently this had been a problem with the Edinburgh Castle from the outset as, unlike pre-war vessels, its decks were sheathed in pitch pine rather than teak. Due to a lack of skilled carpenters at the time it was built the deck planks had not been fitted, just overlayed, and as a result water would seep through, corroding the steel beneath, with the rust then weeping on to the deck. In dry spells the crew would pump red lead paint between the steel plates and wooden planking to prevent the rusting but this was always just a temporary measure and everyone had to get used to the rusting deck.

The Edinburgh Castle was in the main a mail ship, carrying mail from England to South Africa, but it was also a passenger cruise ship which could carry up to 227 first class passengers, 478 cabin class passengers and 400 crew. The accommodation for first class passengers was spacious and had been enjoyed over the years by thousands of British travellers on extended holidays to South Africa. The tourist class accommodation attracted immigrants, students and travellers on a budget. Each of the decks included a lounge, a smoking room, veranda café, dining room and swimming pool for each class of passenger.

The cosmopolitan mix of the passengers, the apparent wealth of those in first class, and the stark contrast of the living conditions on board for the budget traveller, was an eye opener for Harry. He had never witnessed anything like it before. Then again, he had never visited Las Palmas or South Africa, it was all a new and wonderful experience for him.

Harry met a few new mates and spent his time, when not working or sleeping, playing cards and dominoes, drinking rum and whisky and smoking his Senior Service cigarettes. He was enjoying his first voyage as a Merchant Navy seaman and knew he would not always be a bridge boy. Harry wrote a few letters to the people he considered his 'family': Mrs Harvey, Peter and Janet. He missed them all.

CHAPTER SIX

THE BLUE ROOM

NUMBER seven, I think his name was Charles, lay on his bed slowly whimpering, his chest heaving in and out and hot tears were rolling down the cheeks of his reddened, bruised and bloody face. He held the blanket up to his neck, clutching at it with clenched fists, tucking it tightly underneath his chin, as if that thin blanket would protect him from everything within the home and everything in the outside world. His cries were barely audible. He seemed to have reached the point where his crying affected the way he was breathing, catching his breath at each physical, emotional exertion. To see him lying in his bed in the dormitory on his own weeping was not that unusual. The same scene could be witnessed every day of other boys who had taken a severe beating. But as I looked at Charles I knew that something unusual had happened; his head was swollen to twice its normal size. He had taken the most brutal of beatings, but it had not been witnessed by any other of the boys, for Charles had been taken to the most feared of places, the secrets of which were only known by those who had been taken there by staff and who would come out so traumatised they appeared to be in a kind of trance. Charles had been forced into what we boys simply called the 'blue room', as it had a blue door. But what happened behind that door was never talked about, neither by the staff nor the boys who had been forced inside its mysterious walls. When we broke the rules the masters and nuns would threaten to take us to the blue room, and that threat was enough to instil such fear inside us, we would immediately tow the line and do anything the staff asked of us.

The incident with Charles had started in one of the large halls where several of us boys, as we often did, were hard at work polishing the hard wooden floor. We were all given rags which we had to tie to our feet and then move our feet quickly to polish the floor. In any other circumstances, this particular chore could have produced some fun and laughs, with us all apparently dancing in unison, a kind of choreographed cleaning regime – but not in St Mary's where laughter was never heard and smiling was out of place. As we stood shaking our legs, making circles on the floor with the rags on our feet, some of the staff, to amuse themselves and to feed their sadistic tendencies, would slide a heavy floor cleaning block we called a 'dummy' across the polished floor, sending one of the boys crashing to the ground, often banging their heads heavily in the process. It was like they were playing a game of bowls and we boys were the skittles. Except this was not a game of fun, it was for staff to exercise their power and control over the boys. In short, it was cruelty to children, clear and violent physical abuse.

This is what had happened to Number Seven, Charles, who was a thin boy, with little strength in his body. He was polishing the floor, like the rest of us, when one of the grinning male staff sent the 'dummy' sliding across the floor at speed. The heavy block knocked Charles off his feet in an instant and when he came down he came down hard, his head smashing on the dense wooden surface. I can still hear the crack now. His head split open and blood slowly spilled on to the floor and Charles became hysterical, screaming as if he was close to death. But rather than comfort him and tend to his wounds the staff shouted at him to shut up, calling him a 'soft lad', a 'mummy's boy' and when he wouldn't calm down they threatened him with the blue room. He was still hysterical, so they pulled him up from the floor and off they went with him, only for Charles to return an hour or so later when he was placed in his bed in the dormitory, with a small bandage, cut from a white bed sheet, wrapped around his bloody head. It was plain for anyone to see that Charles was in need of medical attention, but he lay there for hours, in agony, before a doctor arrived. The doctor gave him a clean bandage, an injection, and then left him. No one outside the secretive walls of St Mary's Home would find out about Charles and his swollen head. Just like no one mentioned the ever-present bruises on the faces, arms and legs of the boys. If anything was said it was put down to our own boisterous behaviour, boys will be boys, or an accident. No one ever questioned or challenged the excuses given for our injuries, because no one really cared.

I personally cannot recall being sexually molested, the only thing I recall is waking up during the night and being shocked to see a man's face looking down at me. The face appeared to look big and it was a very white face, the colour of that faced looked as though it was similar to a very thin mask, or it could have been

some kind of white make up. I remember being absolutely terrified. Then within a few seconds I saw the figure of a person
quickly moving away. That image has stayed with me to this day,
often surfacing to make me ponder over and over again about it,
whether I had been sexually assaulted I cannot be sure, but I feel
that had I not woken up something would have happened to me
because why would someone be at my bedside in those circumstances in the middle of the night? I could easily exaggerate the
situation by saying that I was assaulted, but I would rather tell the
truth.

Some of the staff, as I have mentioned before, appeared to be
obsessed by sex. Perhaps they were sexually repressed? When the
boys came out of the showers we had to stand naked in front of
at least two members of staff, we were told to lift our arms up
above our heads then told to turn around, then after a few seconds
we could wrap a towel around us, we could then get dried and
dressed. This happened every time we got a shower. I now think
to myself, what was that all about? Why was it that before a boy
was given a beating he would always be stripped naked, and why
did these evil bastards force all the other children to watch – what
was all that about? Why was it that many times when going to the
toilet during the night there would be a nun standing looking
down on the dark stair case, not making a sound just standing
there as still as stone and looking down?

The nun always seemed to be there standing still, looking
down, she was not wearing her big white head gear and I remember the shock of noting that she was completely bald. I must say
it was very spooky indeed, I only went for a number one, but
ended up having a number two. That nun stood so still with the
black gown they wear, I still used to think it was a ghost. After
using the toilet I remember trying not to look up those dark stairs.
I would run like hell back into the dormitory with my little heart
pounding. I now understand why so many of the younger ones
would rather run the risk of peeing in the bed knowing that they
would be thrown into a freezing bath, which was the punishment
for bed wetting. I have been told that I sometimes have a dark
sense of humour, I sometimes wonder if this dark side of my
nature has something to do with those blackening tins on which I
lay upon in my pram when I was just a small baby of four months.

Another of the boys, Number Eight, had been summonsed into

an office by the masters after they discovered he had been walking with and talking to a girl on his way back to the Home from school. They asked him all sorts of perverted questions, like had he touched the girl, had he thought about touching the girl, where on her body had he thought about touching her, had these thoughts led to any changes in his body? Fucking perverts. They then threatened him with the 'Blue Room' and ordered him never to speak to the girl again. They said that they would be talking to the girl's mother, to make sure to put a stop to either something happening or developing between the two of them. What they had done was stifle Number Eight's first opportunity to mix with a girl, and perhaps develop his first romance. On the outside in civvy street, such meetings between boys and girls of our age were both innocent and natural, but in the walls of St Mary's every innocent and 'normal' incident could be turned into something dirty, something sinful and wrong.

The 'Blue Room' was only talked about in whispers between the boys and it had a fearful reputation. I once tried to talk to one of the boys who had been subjected to a visit to the 'Blue Room', but he would shake terribly and then burst out crying. It worried me as his face would turn as white as a sheet. I never found out what went on in the 'Blue Room' and decided that I would never ask.

Abuse of children was so rife in just about all Catholic Institutions around the world, that decade after decade cases of serious abuse were being uncovered, abuse perpetrated by priests, nuns, choir masters and other staff employed within Catholic Institutions. How could this happen on such a massive scale and continue for so long? It is a question that I have tried to unravel, especially with myself being a victim. One thing that I have observed was that the abusers within an orphanage and such institutions are 'single' people who live within the actual premises of the places they worked. In my experience in the so called 'care' homes none of the staff had normal relationships. Was frustration one of the factors that shaped their way of thinking? It is common knowledge that priests and nuns are (supposedly) celibate, not only are they doomed to a loveless life in the adult sense, marriage etc., according to the doctrine of their religion, it is deemed to be a sin for them to ever think of, or desire that normal people take for granted. If they do break the rule of desiring a member of the opposite sex they are committing the sin of lust, it is also a serious offence for them to masturbate, and in my opinion, masturbation is just nature's way of giving human beings an alternative way of releasing sexual tension and frustration.

The importance of masturbation for all, who are unable to ease the sexual tension with a partner, can be seen in prison. Can you imagine the chaos it would create if prisoners, both male and female, did not have any way of releasing the sexual tension? Well that's exactly the situation with these abusers of children in the Catholic Institutions they find themselves in and I believe that it is because of such restrictions and the inability to do what is natural because of their religious beliefs, that can trigger the abusers despicable behaviour towards children. These people are actually attempting to go against nature itself. Catholics, even to this day, are not allowed to practice contraception in any way. Condoms are not allowed: they are told to use a method known as the rhythm method. I believe it is wrong to force such rules upon so many millions of Catholic people – if there is a loving God up there, he or she would not place such rules that go against the very nature that the Almighty himself created. Because an Almighty God would foresee that such restrictions would certainly cause big problems for members of the Catholic Church, problems which would lead to many followers of their rules to lose control of their behaviour leading in turn to horrific crimes against other people, defenceless young children in particular.

What really horrifies me is that now we know that when priests or other members of the Catholic Church were discovered to be abusers, they had a system where an abuser would be seconded to another Church, or institution, rather than being dealt with and prosecuted and even jailed as a criminal. In effect these "criminals" where protected by the top brass of the Church and it really sickens me that I and many other defenceless children had no protection at all. As the decades rolled by more and more serious complaints would be made from all over the world by victims of these evil doers, which resulted in the church having to reluctantly concede that they where indeed guilty of institutionalised wicked behaviour. It is only recently that the head of the Catholic Church the 'POPE' has, with a great deal of reluctance and pressure on him, finally apologised in public for the decades of pure wickedness committed by many members of his flock.

My own personal experiences at the hands of these abusers in St Mary's Home in Tudhoe, County Durham, made me realise that these perpetrators where completely out of control. Most of the people who run places such as orphanages etc, are either total idiots or they are aware of what's going on, it's obvious that children's homes will attract paedophiles, sadists and the like and that abuse of one kind of another will definitely take place. Yet the people at the top who are responsible for the welfare of those in their care contact the orphanage to 'alert' them that there will be a top person arriving for an inspection, anyone who has been in these kinds of situations will corroborate what I am saying. I am not a top man responsible for these institutions, *in fact* I am referred to as a villain. If I were in their position I would eliminate virtually all abuse by just using common sense and a little bit of imagination.

A staged photo of the orphanage children.

I would not alert the staff in any way, I would turn up with a couple of trusted people and I would then take two or three children from the nursery, juniors and seniors. I would let the kids know that they would be going elsewhere, then ask them to let me know how things were, how they were being treated. I know for a fact that if there was such an arrangement like that myself and many children would have been saved from the abuse, from the horrible 'crimes' that we children were submitted to. It is common knowledge that kids will be frightened to talk if they feel that after talking, they would then be put back into the charge of the very same people who were abusing them. This method would leave the perpetrators in a weakened position; he or she could no longer feel free to abuse at will because he or she would be aware that there was now a system in place which would stop them in their tracks. Our abuse could have been avoided, but there was not one person – or 'top person' – who had the brains or imagination to stop these 'criminals'. This picture of myself and the other children really does tell a story, not one of them is smiling, it is merely a staged photograph, the children look frightened and nervous.

St Mary's Catholic Home (which has now been demolished) held many hidden secrets that now may never come to light and I feel sure that there where quite literally skeletons in the cupboards there.

CHAPTER SEVEN

THE BLACK VIRGIN

THE darkness of night had fallen and all the boys were asleep in their dorms, all bar myself and Number Eight, my best friend in the orphanage, Harry Marsden. Harry had found a tin of black paint and we had both decided that we were going to hit the institution hard, right at the core of its very being, by targeting something that the nuns and masters believed symbolised all they and their religious beliefs stood for, the statue of the Virgin Mary.

Harry and I had found ourselves in the so called 'Top Dorm'. As well as the so called Sisters of Mercy there were other staff who worked and lived in the orphanage, and one who stands out above all the others for her cruelty was a woman called Miss Malone. She was in charge of the Top Dorm and she lived for no other reason than to dish out pain.

By this time Harry and I were getting older and more worldly-wise and we shared a deep hatred for the orphanage, the people who ran it and the Roman Catholic religion they followed with such zeal. We had taken so many beatings that pain meant nothing to either Harry or I and we were always on the lookout for any way we could get back at these absolute bastards. When Harry by chance found the tin of black paint we discussed what we should do with it and we both agreed we should use it to leave our mark somewhere, let the bastards know we were young, free spirits, that their abuse might cause us pain, but they couldn't take away our individuality. I suggested to Harry we should paint the Virgin Mary and, at first, he just laughed his head off. When it dawned on him I was serious, we set a plan to strike. That night we crept out of our beds like two little SAS soldiers. Taking care not to make a sound we made our way out and up onto the roof. It was a pitch dark night and as we got onto the roof I remember looking up at the stars wishing that I was there and not here. We knew that the most sacred thing that the nuns had was this statue of the Virgin Mary. To us it was just a symbol of all the pain of kneeling in the yard praying every morning and the pleading for forgiveness that we had to make: the piece of stone stood motionless whilst we had to endure the beatings and abuse forced on us.

The colour of this statue was blue and white and that night Harry and I painted it black, the colour that represents evil. We felt really great about it and after admiring our handy work we sneaked back in the Top Dorm, under the sleeping nose of the supervisor, and went to bed. We just couldn't wait until we were marched into the yard to pray the next morning, and found it hard to sleep.

The next morning the nuns and Miss Malone got us all up at 5am and the same everyday routine followed; beds checked, cold baths, then out into the yard for our solemn morning prayers. No one was allowed to look up at the statue until the order was given. When it was time to look the shock on the faces of the sisters and the other staff was plain for all to see. Some were screaming and some were even crying. Within a few seconds, after the staff discovered the tell-tale evidence of bits of black paint on our hands, Harry and I were dragged, kicked and punched into the main building.

We both took one hell of a beating, but not without having a go back this time, we battled well and they had to get the male staff in to help them overpower us. We were dragged into the office where there was a big table. Our clothes were literarily ripped from our bodies and they then spread eagled us face down on the table. They tied us down one by one and whipped us with the birch. Whilst this was going on Sister Kevin constantly screamed at us to cry, but we would not give them the satisfaction of seeing us crying. Her face was full of nothing less than hatred for us, but we would not cry. This made the situation worse as they continued to flog the hell out of us. We were then dragged to the same old bath for the cold bath treatment. Harry and I were black and blue from head to foot, but deep inside we were over the moon, knowing just how much we had hurt them.

We were both kept off school, simply because of the state we were in. They didn't want anyone to see what they had done to us. We had to stay off school for two weeks, but this was not for rest, we had to do hard labour every day. During the two weeks we had to slog it out, most of this time spent in what was nothing less than excruciating and severe pain from the beatings doled out to us. Harry planned another escape, this time it was his plan to run and run for good, and eventually he got his chance.

One night he just up and left. He climbed over Miss Malone's cubicle which was at the end of the dormitory, grabbed his clothes and found some money which he took with him, he then climbed out of the dormitory window and shinned it down the drainpipe, and he was off once again. This time he clambered down to the River Wear, but he made the mistake of going to a shop close at hand and the wife in the shop realised he was from the orphanage. She phoned the police and once again he was back in the home. He was by now under the belief that they couldn't do any more harm to him than that which they had already done. Ok they might lock him up in the old wooden chest, but again he was used to that now. They did the usual beating, haircut, cold bath and the old wooden trunk but it only made Harry all the more determined to get out.

We were by this time quite literally past caring and Harry and I got up to all kinds of trouble, especially at school. We would be up for anything, fighting was our main thing. One thing about the homes – you did learn to fight – so beating up on the outside lads was just normal to us. Harry and I did have one real outside pal though, his name was Nipper O'Connor. He would bring us food into school, plus there was a shop on the way to school called The Dairy, that's were Harry learnt to shoplift. You have to understand we were starving in the orphanage; you would even see lads pinching bread from the hens, who incidentally were fed better than we were.

There was another incident that sticks out in my mind, one of the young girl workers had been out on the town, but she must have been followed back, because we were woken up by a man trying to get into her room. With the racket we raised he fled and the next evening after tea some of us sneaked knives out of the dining hall, but when we were lined up for bed I guess someone had informed on us. We were searched and those of us with knives were kept behind whilst the rest went to bed. We took the knives thinking this guy would come back that night.

Once again we were taken into the office and stripped and then tied to the same table and whipped once again with this birch. But this time they went overboard and punches rained down on us. We both were to face some terrible beatings in the years ahead, but this will always stand out above all. Harry was flogged so badly he had to be confined to bed for nearly four weeks. Those bastards got away with fucking murder. What chance did he or we have?

We had no one to tell, no one to run to, our only weapon against these evil bastards was to take the pain. Now nothing could hurt us. When Harry used to talk about this he would say 'I was rejected by my parents, the fucking Sisters hated me, and the school hated me and you really didn't get the chance to make any friends', so really you felt totally alone, stuck and lost in the wilderness. Even Nipper O'Connor was really only our friend out of fear. At this stage Harry would be coming up to eleven years of age, when you reached eleven here you were moved from the Top Dormitory to the seniors.

As for the whipping over the knives, Harry was laid up in bed for four weeks, and then he was able to return back to school. Harry would have been on his toes by that time, but they were keeping a good eye on him. They didn't let him anywhere near his clothes, they kept them well out of the way, plus on top of this one of the staff would always be around watching him. Well it was back on the punishment runs to and from school, the guy who took us was called Mick Demerrick, even till this day I can see his face, and honest I swear you could chop sticks with it, all his features were pointed, he looked a ringer for Fagan the *Oliver Twist* guy. On my second run we were coming up to what we called the four lane ends, as we neared it Harry suddenly took off down the lane and did not stop running until his lungs were ready to burst.

The dormitories that we slept in were nothing less than draconian, rows of beds and in between these a very long rusty metal locker. I can still hear the screams of the kids being beaten during the night after they had been dragged to the drill hall or cellar.

For learning we had to march to an outside school, this in a line of twos. The school treated us like third class beings, they knew that we were from St Mary's orphanage and obviously knew that we had nobody to turn to. They always treated us differently from ordinary pupils, it was also terrible listening to the other children when they spoke about their lives and their families, we quite simply just had nothing, absolute nothing to look forward to from day to day and it hurt us all deeply when we heard them talking about their lives outside school. Though this was very hard to bear it was still better than being stuck in St Mary's Orphanage all day. The worst bit about school was going back to St Mary's at the end of the school day where we knew the slightest mistake would cause us much more pain and suffering.

In the orphanage yard if the bell rang out we had to drop to our knees and pray to the Virgin Mary. By painting the statue black Harry and I had sent a message to those in authority and to the system, a message from all the boys in the home, we hated them all.

CHAPTER EIGHT

SON OF SATAN

VERONICA was just what Harry Marsden needed. She taught him how to kiss properly, to 'neck on' and I remember him telling me that at first he was very shy, but eventually he felt all grown up. This lass was from Middlesbrough and Harry and her met up later in life. To Harry all this kissing was great, but then just as quick he was back again in school. Veronica, who worked in the orphanage, would bring her friend along, who also worked in the home in the nursery. Her name was Marlene and she was also from Middlesbrough. She was seeing a lad at the time, let's just say his name was Tommy Gee, and Harry would meet up with them on the cricket field on our way to school. He could wag off school as they would not miss him, thinking he was off unwell.

Harry told me that one nice summer's day he was lying down with Veronica out of the sight of the other two and all of a sudden, Veronica grabbed his hand and slipped it inside her top. Well he just froze and hell came flooding through his head, he really thought that she understood what he was going through, because she kept telling him to relax and not to be afraid. She was really good at helping him. Sure they had sex, but he was far too afraid and tense, he went on to say that he felt really awful. Back in the orphanage Harry was beside himself with guilt. He thought every-one was looking at him and I recall him saying that he dared not look at any of the Sisters, simply because he felt really ashamed. I am sure he felt the wrath of hell burning his arse. Things really did get better for Harry and he really had fallen in love with this girl. He had always had girlfriends at school and I think that it was because we were always in some kind of trouble. I remember Harry being made up when two of them called him their hero. For Harry this Veronica was special, while those at school were just girlfriends.

Harry and I hated the teachers at school just as much as the Sisters of Mercy. I remember we were on our way to school one day, a few of us lads including Fatty D and George P. Harry found on the way this barrel of oil and decided to cover Fatty and George's hands and face with it. When they got to school and the teachers saw them, all hell broke out. They were marched back to the orphanage. This was one thing that Harry regretted doing because Sister Kevin, Sister Mary and Sister Lucy got two men, Mr Donnelly, the home gardener, and Mr Boss, to punish those who needed punishing.

They held Harry down whilst the Sisters took a big scrubbing brush and carbolic soap and scrubbed his face until it was red raw. George P was a bit slow, not the full shilling, but he was not a complete idiot. A couple of days later he wanted to run away, so he sat down with Harry and talked about it and they both agreed they would go. To get away they needed some money, and Harry knew just the place to get it. During the night, not long after check up, both of them got up and crept to the cupboard were our Sunday clothes were usually kept, then climbed out of the building.

George had decided he wanted to kill one of the Sisters if not all three, so Harry and George went into the kitchen and grabbed a knife each. They then crept into Sister Lucy's room, which was nearest to the kitchen, and she was lying in bed all dressed in white. Harry and George crept up to her bed and stood over her and Harry raised his knife over her and I remember him saying that he was really going to kill her, but he just couldn't bring himself to bring that knife down on her. A few years later Harry told me that he honestly wanted to kill her, but swears to this day that something was holding him back; he wanted her dead because he was so full of hatred, but his arms would not move. Suddenly without her even opening her eyes and in a very quiet voice she said 'go back to bed', he told me that they just could not get out of that room fast enough.

Harry and George did eventually escape and made their way to their homes. George knocked on the door and his mother shouted 'who's there', George answered back 'mum its me your son', well the answer he got back was 'fuck off back to the home, I don't want you, why do you think I put you in there', then this guy opened the door and both George and Harry ran off. Harry remembers that night it was very cold, so they searched several back yards together for anything that would keep them warm, they then crawled into someone's outside toilet, but with it being so cold it was impossible for them to sleep. To cap everything off George started to cry uncontrollably. Harry recalled that he couldn't believe it, George started saying that he was to blame for him running away. I guess he was starting to panic on what was going to happen when they ended back at the home.

When Harry was telling me, he said he just completely lost the plot and started to give George a hiding with a large piece of wood. He swore later that he thought he had left him for dead. Harry just left him there covered with blood and he thought it's no good heading for Newcastle, because his mother would just hand him over to the police, so he headed back in the direction of the home. Not too far from the home there was a place named St Charles Catholic School, and not far from the school there were some hills and from these you could see all the coming's and going's around the school. Harry made himself a makeshift camp and settled there. During the day he was outside of the school and grabbed a couple of outsiders who were really scared of us, he told them to get some bedding and food brought in at dinner time, they did and he then told them to get a message to me.

Well the inevitable happened and I ended up on the run again with Harry. Our little camp was becoming a real home, we would go out at night and nick what clothes we could, plus we had become very good at shoplifting as well. He would distract the shopkeeper, or I would, so we would always manage to keep ourselves fed, plus we would sneak back into the orphanage's hen hut and take what eggs were there. We had just about everything we needed. We would light up a fire and boil our eggs in a bucket, we even had toast and boiled potatoes, which we stole from the fields. What a great life it was and to think that this was going to be our home forever, or so we thought.

Most if not all of the outside lads – those who weren't living at the orphanage – were in fear of us. Looking back I would say we were running a school and orphanage protection racket, but like all good things, our plans on the run did not always go according to plan. So it turned out we got surrounded by police and Harry was fully questioned about his attack on George, because he had received quite a few head stitches, but he stood his ground and swore that he had not attacked him, so in the end they let the sisters and staff deal with him and I. So once again we had to run the gauntlet, but like always we gave them a run for their money.

The only way to beat these people was to never scream out, or cry. Certain things went on then that I and Harry didn't understand about at that time, but now I look back and realise that some of the vulnerable lads were being sexually abused. On many occasions Mr Boss would get certain lads up out of their beds and take them to his cubicle through the night. You would hear these lads pleading 'please sir don't' and some of these lads would be sobbing all night, even after he took them back to bed. Others would get little bits of perks from him, but like I say, how could we know at that time what was going on? So very often boys would cry out when being punished, but now we realise what this evil pervert was doing how the hell he wanted. I don't know how these awful people could get away with so very much.

Well Harry got the inevitable punishment for his escapade, but again after a few weeks he was back at school as normal, although there was nothing normal about this place. One day on his way to school he, along with Fatty Dougal and this other lad whose name slips me by, were on their way to school and they went by this disused railway line and on each side of this line the banks were covered in bracken. Well Harry set light to it and scampered off to school. Whilst he was sitting in class the fire engines went flying by and he did not know then the extent of the damage he had caused. He later found out that it went into thousands of pounds, because several telephone poles were burnt down. On top of all this the traffic was stopped and many houses had to be evacuated. What Harry didn't know was that he had been seen by two girls, who had already reported him.

A lad came into the class and spoke to the teacher Miss Kelly and said that the Headmaster, Mr Hanratty, wanted Harry to go to his office right away. Harry told me that when he got there he was made to wait outside with two male staff and then a few minutes later the police walked into the school. He was questioned for hours, but kept on saying it was not him who had done the deed. Well obviously, do you think they believed him, like hell they did, he was taken to Spennymoor Police Station. At this time I was on the run with six other lads.

The police kept him for hours, they even locked him up in a cell and kept him there all night. They kept the lights on and banged on the door periodically all night just to keep him awake. Well he ended up on a charge of arson; no one else got charged, just Harry, because he told them it was him and him only. He was remanded back to the home. He was welcomed by the staff who started beating him up in front of the police. When Harry told me this he also said he remembered the police going out of the home laughing whilst the staff dragged him around the floor by his hair. They pulled lumps out of his head, then he was thrown bodily into the cold bath, worse still he remembers one of the Sisters shouting "drown the evil son of Satan, drive the devil out of him." They kept him in that bath for hours. He was then dragged naked and shivering into a lobby and made to kneel in front of a painting of the Virgin Mary. They had a priest there, Father Cane, who started chucking Holy Water on him. He realised these nuns really believed that Harry was possessed by the devil. Father Cane did not care for me either, because the summer before, both Harry and I raided his orchard for apples: he came rushing out in a rage to catch us, but he tripped and broke two of his fingers and sure we got the obligatory hiding then as well.

Well special occasions, they come and go, a special time was Easter. Usually, we had to pray like there was no tomorrow, we had to endure everything they wanted us to endure, without question or without any kind of emotion. Easter was different though, Woolworth's, the big shop on the High Street, would send us something very special. A gigantic Easter egg would arrive and would be put on show for us all to look at. The big day would arrive and we would all watch expectantly drooling from the lips as they broke this up, sneaking the odd piece for themselves in the process, then as we trooped passed they handed out a small piece of chocolate to the 250 boys waiting in the line. If you got a piece bigger than a half penny then everyone thought you were the luckiest of the lucky.

Despite the threats of severe punishment being doled out by some of the cruel sadistic staff, some of the boys in St Mary's Orphanage did lose their boyish tempers. Like all institutions bullying was a way of life and did go on, it's no small wonder that children lost their tempers and consequently used violence upon each other. I was reminded quite recently, by an ex St Mary's Orphanage boy, that he always remembers that I used to protect him from the bigger and stronger boys (bullies). Although I cannot remember much about the bully boys in St Mary's Orphanage I do recall one incident that I have never been able to forget to this day. I cannot remember the exact details of why this incident took place, but I do remember the incident or should I say the 'violence' itself. I can remember that by this time I was about 14 years of age and I was in what they called the seniors section. The incident took place just outside an area called the work room. The boy's first name I can remember clearly though and he was called Danny, he was by all accounts a big thick set strapping lad, but he wore glasses. We were arguing about something of which I cannot recall now, but what I do remember is that I just lost it and snapped. I hit him so very hard in the face, or should I say in the spectacles. Danny screamed with pain and I can remember hitting him again and again eventually knocking him to the ground. In those days and certainly in this place, once an opponent was down they were given the chance to get up and continue to fight, but there was no getting up for Danny. His glasses were broken and there was blood seeping from one of his eyes. I quietly slipped away from the work room area, but later learned that Danny had lost almost all of the vision from one eye, needless to say I was caught and two of the male staff took me over to the sister superiors office on a charge of fighting. I was told to stay off school as a result of this and was forced to work in the building (doing hard labour) for the next few days. At that point no one was aware that Danny would or could lose the sight of one of his eyes, it was merely looked upon as a fight between two boys. Very soon after the incident though Danny just vanished. He just left the orphanage, he was by then around 15 years of age, and he had in effect served his time in that dreadful place. I have never seen or heard from him since and I often wonder what became of him. Danny though, at that time, was just nothing less than a down right bully and as I got older I was the one who through this kind of experience ended up having a deep hatred and total dislike for bullies and all of their kind, consequently I have thrashed a lot of them over the years, either in borstal or in prison, or out on the streets.

I mention this, what would be now considered more than just an incident, because I feel that it must have been the start of my philosophy of forever sticking up for the weak, or the underdog. I now realize that I was nothing less than a very confused and bitter young boy when I left St Mary's. I had then and still have nothing less than a wicked temper. I am just incapable and unable to argue without losing control, I just seem to 'snap' and become what many of my friends refer to as almost insane, although this is only for a short time. I then calm down and always regret what I have done, not so much for the victims of my temper, but because I had quite literally lost control of myself. I feel that losing control of oneself is not a very wise thing to do and to this day that temper of mine is always simmering within me like a mini volcano. My bad temper is one of the biggest factors as to why I have had no other choice but to live on my own.

It's not normal for anyone to completely explode into violence quite literally at the drop of a hat and for the slightest of reasons. I have always been like a walking time bomb. It really is quite frightening and indeed it is 'dangerous' for any man or woman that takes that one step and challenges me in the slightest way – they are then immediately attacked. The only way I can resolve this problem is to live on my own and as a further result of this I only very rarely leave the sanctuary of my own house. The puzzling thing is that despite the above many of my friends and people who have taken the time to get to know me refer to me as a canny lad, sometimes I think they mean I canny keep my temper.

What made me this way? Well reading this book will help you to understand why I am this way, if nothing else St Mary's Orphanage did have a profound effect on my life, it certainly moulded me into what I was to become and the way I behave. If things had been different or indeed if we had been given even a little of the respect we needed or deserved, or more importantly the counselling when we really needed it, things might have or could have turned out a lot better for everyone.

Wherever I have been, and whoever I was with during the chaos of my life, I have been both incapable and unable to feel the slightest bit happy or have any sense of what is referred to by many as the Christmas Spirit. It has always puzzled me as to why and how people appear to anticipate with the greatest of joy and happiness what is known as the Christmas period. I just don't get it, believe me though I have tried my best to get into the Christmas buzz, but to absolutely no avail. To be perfectly honest I cannot remember a great deal about any Christmas whilst growing up as a child in St Mary's Orphanage, or Tudhoe Home as many call it, and after talking to survivors of that wretched place they further remind me that there was very little change to the mundane work routine during the Christmas period – which is obviously why that I do not recall much at all about Christmas.

Another thing that I recall is that for all the years I spent in the homes only one boy passed the eleven plus exam, I began to dwell on that statistic and pondered the question why should this be and I came to the conclusion that it was a psychological problem. I studied the photo of myself and the other kids in the staged photograph in this book. Anyone seeing that photo will immediately see that all the kids shown in it are extremely unhappy, unwanted, unloved, and above all frightened. I do not think that kids in that mental state or mind set would be able to concentrate or enjoy school in any way. We kids felt different, we felt and indeed we were treated as outcasts; education was the last thing on our minds. What was on our minds was the horror of the floggings we had received or had witnessed the night before.

What was in our minds all day was the question, would I be the victim of their brutality when we got back to the home after school? We would be terrified that a teacher would contact the home reporting something negative, small things that you may not have done, which would end up with some other unfortunate child or yourself being severely punished? With a mind set like that it is little wonder that just about all the kids in that so called 'care home' had severe learning difficulties, we were under extreme stress all of the time. In my school report it states that I was well mannered, I was not well mannered in the normal sense I was extremely frightened – it was 'fear' not good manners. I know for a fact that the schoolteachers knew what was going on in that horrible place; they would see the evidence of this right in front of their eyes. Kids sitting in front of them with injuries, they witnessed that on many occasions. One only had to look into the eyes of the children, they were eyes of shock and fear, but we had absolutely no one to turn to, every one turned a blind eye, the teachers, the doctors and everyone was the same. As far as I was concerned they all pissed in the same bucket, they were all guilty, the whole system let us down, they went to their graves and were spoken of as pillars of society, when in fact many were evil people. If there is such a thing as hell, that is were they will be, and that is where they should be if there is any justice in this world.

CHAPTER NINE
THE RELEASE

EVERY morning there was mass at the orphanage, despite the fact we had already kneeled before the Virgin Mary in the courtyard to say very early morning prayers. After the mass, which seemed to go on forever, we would then be taken to the dining hall for breakfast. I always remember being very hungry, because we were fed so very little. Our usual meal was a bowl of gruel, which was actually watered down porridge, this being accompanied with a slice of dry and often stale bread. After breakfast we were simply put to work, polishing the floor with our feet until it looked like glass, or other chores. Myself, Harry and the others would ask ourselves: "is this what we were born for?" Is this what life is all about? Does this mean we have to stay here and do this for the rest of our lives? But mainly we wondered why?

After morning chores we were then taken to get ready for school. The school was three miles from the Orphanage and we had to walk it in all weathers, four times a day marching in two lines of two and believe me it was hard, or so we thought until we started being put on the punishment line. Most of us found school no better than the orphanage, because the teachers would often single us out. It was just so simple and easy for them to vent their anger on us, simply because we had no parents to turn to. We found from an early age, whether it was in the orphanage or inside school, that we would often be singled out and blamed for just about everything that came to mind. It did not matter whether or not you were innocent, the mere implication that you might be was enough for them to punish you, this without any chance of stating your case. In the end most of us just gave up and went out of our way to get into as much trouble as we could, at least that way we would be getting punished for a reason. In school our first lesson would be prayers, then other lessons, which both Harry and I had no interest at all in.

At dinner time we would then be marched back again to the orphanage for our dinner. We would be given a bowl of cabbage water, which was totally vile, but we had to drink it. We also got a slice of bread to go with it, but again it was always hard and often had green bits sticking out of it.

Going back to school for the afternoon and then back to our living hell at the end of the school day was bad enough but what made it worse was having to jog the three miles each way four times a day in hard heavy boots with no socks. This gave us all blisters which would burst open and sometimes bleed and it hurt, but we were passed crying. This was the punishment line for those who had broken the rules, and there were many of us. We would be kept on this punishment until the nuns and the sadistic staff thought that we had learned our lesson. Most lads in the home quickly accepted defeat, but Harry, like me, did not give a fuck about their rules and regulations. The nuns and staff would then give us some exercise to work off the heavenly dinner. We would again go back to the cloth on the feet and polishing of the floor, then it was the three mile hike back to school. No sooner than school was over in the afternoon, we were marching the three miles back to our living hell. When we got back to the orphanage our tea consisted of a bowl of semolina and by this time another slice of what was even staler bread and, if we were lucky, a piece of cheese would be dropped in front of us. Things rarely changed from day to day. After tea we would be put back to work and if lucky, we would be let out into the yard for a bit of play, under the constant gaze of the nuns.

Many things stand out in my mind that were to ready me for my life ahead. One thing I learned was to accept pain and I learned not to cry, or to scream out.

When Harry was AWOL and camped in the woods a crowd of grown ups would gather on a Saturday and play pitch and toss with two pennies. These would be thrown into the air and people would then gamble on how they would land, this was illegal so these guys always needed lookouts. Harry used to get a half penny or if he was lucky a penny, which in those days was worth a lot. Eventually the police were tipped off and they raided the woods and captured Harry. When the police had left after dropping him back at the orphanage the Sisters of Charity stripped him naked, shaved his head to the bone with the old blunt scissors and dragged him off to the freezing bath. He was then caned severely and then locked up in the old wooden chest. He told me years later that this was really scary, it was pitch black and he could not move, he was left there for a very long time – to Harry it must have seemed like an eternity. Eventually we had to line up again whilst they opened the wooden chest and pulled him out, he could hardly stand up, obviously suffering from severe cramp. They dragged him out into the yard and made him kneel facing the statue of the Virgin Mary still looking down from the roof. They started to beat him saying: "Repent, ask the Virgin Mary for forgiveness". Eventually, after what seemed like a life time, he did.

Harry then was told to put on his clothes, his shorts and a pair of boots, but no socks, and the nuns gave him the dreaded Red Jumper, to show everyone that he was being punished. Harry, like me, was going to have to get used to these items because we would rarely be out of them during our time at St Mary's Orphanage, these were what was known as the punishment clothes. Whilst on punishment we were made to work non stop and to make matters worse we were made to wear the punishment clothes whilst going to school and a man, who worked in the orphanage, would ride alongside us on a bike as we were made to jog in a row to school. I and many will never forget the people who lived on this three mile route to the school; they would always be at their gates, the gates to their nice little homes waiting to see who was in the line. At school we were made to sit on our own, separated from the others.

This kind of treatment in many ways took away something from us, sure it made us tough and sure it made us bend to the establishment, the nuns owned us lock stock and barrel. Living in this environment often meant that we took out our frustrations unfairly on those around us, but they had an answer for that as well. If we were caught fighting one another, no matter what the reason, they would put us into the boxing ring in the gym to finish the matter. Of course they had rules on this, it was get in there and fight it out between you. It took me a long time to realise that boxers wore gloves, we didn't get these and you can bet if you ended up here it hurt. Later in life, Harry was to give a lot to boxing and ultimately before his death he ended up in Buckingham Palace getting an honour from their nibs. He, like so many of us, learned the hard way: 'put up or give up' either way somebody had to come off worse. Yes, the staff and, unbelievably, the Sisters of Charity loved this spectacle.

I don't know where they found some of the staff for this little part of Hell, but they enjoyed, no that's not correct, they absolutely relished their work. They didn't give a hoot for us, they looked on us as 'persona non grata', a person who for some reason is not wanted or welcome. The staff who lived in the little cubicles at the end of each dormitory obviously had it in for us. If we answered them back for any reason, or not in the manner that they liked, they would throw a large bunch of keys or whatever was at hand at us. If you were hit, you dare not cry because that meant punishment, but by this time many of us were way beyond showing any feelings.

I can only recall a couple of things regarding the Christmas period in the orphanage. I do remember once being given a jigsaw puzzle, there were three pieces missing. I remember thinking "the cruel bastards, what do they think this is all about?" I have also been reminded that anything we children got in that terrible place was given to the orphanage by some sort of so called charity, it was obviously second hand which explains the missing pieces of my jigsaw. I can also recall my mate Harry crying all day because he received a so called cowboy outfit that had no guns and no hat, all this cowboy outfit consisted of was some sort of tight fitting waist coat and some thing that went over his knees, we later in life used to laugh and joke about it. I said to him one day that if he had received the 'Full Monty' cowboy outfit with a horse and all, he could have buggered off into the sunset to try and find them three missing pieces of that bloody damned jigsaw of mine. If he had found them, we and all the other children in that place could rejoice by singing ding dong merrily on high, but it was not to be. I know it may appear to be silly but I have always felt vexed about those missing pieces, and I often think the horrible staff did those things to us for their own sadistic and warped amusement. I would not have put it past them, and as for Harry the only time he got close to anything like a cowboy gun was years later when an informant stuck one up against his head, luckily for him though the little arse hole did not have the bottle to use it.

Christmas at the orphanage, like everything else there, left its mark on me. Without any doubt I have always found it very uncomfortable being surrounded by a 'family' and having a

67

Christmas dinner. I always felt elated and happy when it was over. I now realise that we kids in that place had never experienced family gatherings, because we never had a family, so at the end of the day it's hardly surprising. I have just never been able to relate to such things, which is why I have failed at being a proper family man, there are literally too many pieces of the jigsaw of my life missing, these from my psychic or mindset which are now lost for ever. They say one does not miss what one has never had, but I feel that it really is a human right, a human necessity, for a child to at least have the basic in love and care, that which shapes a child's whole life. Even animals suckling their young need that, and the answer to the above question, as far as the rulers of St Mary's Orphanage were concerned, was "No they really did not know it was Christmas", nor did it bother them – not in the slightest. If you ever had a jigsaw that you donated to charity with three pieces missing, then be warned you had better keep this information to yourself, don't tell anyone especially some cowboy riding out of the sunset on a wooden clothes horse waving a gun in the air.

Over the years I have been asked what religion are you Mario? Well my reply has always been: "I don't know". I have not made my mind up, just because I was labelled, or should I say burdened, with the tag of being a 'Catholic' does not mean that I am a 'Catholic'. I belong to no organization. I am myself, and that is the way I want to be. I am not a follower of anyone, I am not part of anyone's 'flock', nor do I belong to anyone as I do not and have never wished to follow another person's doctrine. I am in essence a free spirit and have never blindly followed another's rules – don't class me as being a sheep in anyone's 'flock'. I am a human being, I am myself and I also feel uneasy when I see how many people freely and without thought become members of, almost literally, a shepherd's flock. I find it difficult to understand why people throw themselves into the cultures of any institution or organization, then blindly and automatically urge and indeed condition their own offspring into following their blind faith. With other people I believe that those who believe that there is an almighty God must surely also realize that the God they believe created them also gave them the ability to think for themselves. I feel that religion should be a very private thing that one keeps to one's self and if it was done in that way it would be a lot more potent and sincere.

Wedding of Mario's daughter Andrea to Lee Gabriel at Gretna Green

When people become followers of other people's doctrines it is exactly what it means, followers, it is not their religion. It is someone else's that they are from 2000 years ago copying, it does not appear to be genuine, and it belongs to someone else. I feel that these very large groups of followers can be menacing and indeed dangerous as we are too well aware of the atrocities that such groups can cause. It does not make sense to me, as I am one person and I am an individual. If there is an Almighty Creator he or she actually created me that way and I feel that whatever I believe in is an extremely private and precious thing to me, as an individual I feel very comfortable with my outlook concerning such matters. I have comfort in the knowledge that I am in control of such a very private thing, I also believe that it would be better and a safer world if we kept such things to ourselves. However, I am a realist – I know that my philosophy on the subject can and will never happen, it can never happen because of human nature itself.

The family members at the wedding.

Yes indeed we are all different, some of us are strong in mind some are weak, some of us are born with the ability to see things in a more balanced way than others, and so it goes on, it does not mean that one person is better than another. It is fate, it is simply the way things are, if there is an Almighty Creator I would love to shake his or her hand and congratulate this Almighty being because for one single being to have the power to create a world and universe and all the creatures who roam this universe is an unimaginable and fantastic thing to do. If we knew for sure that this divine being existed every single human being would bow in honour as we would realise that we, at the end of our lives, would be going to meet our maker. The problem is that we cannot be sure that this God exists, all people can do is hope and believe in what in a sense is a dream. Some people actually have such belief in the existence of God that they devote their whole short life to the dream, they literally become followers of a dream. I find it very difficult to understand why so many millions upon millions of people all over the globe have such a one way view of where we come from, where we are, and where we go when we depart from this life. It is truly amazing, a large percentage of the people of the world are following the same dream. I feel that people believe in this dream, not because it really makes sense to believe in what may not exist, they believe it gives them hope and it gives them God, heaven, etc. It's what they want it to be.

For millions of people it is difficult for them to contemplate the possibility that after death there may be nothing. People find it hard to accept that their life will end for eternity. It is people clinging to life. I have to concede that it is part of human nature to do so, but despite all I have said I still cannot go with the flow, I do feel more comfortable and in control by keeping my thoughts on what I may or may not believe to myself. I am not a follower of other people's belief and if the millions of followers feel comfortable with what they believe then good luck to them, for to believe in a better life after death must be very comforting to the mind and it must help in coming to terms with the burdens of life – by leaning on an invisible crutch. I am myself neither a leader nor a follower, I am what I am and I believe that a large percentage of our lives are dictated by fate and circumstances which are things that are beyond our control.

I am a creature influenced by the environment in which I grew up as a child, and that environment was for me St Mary's Orphanage in Tudhoe, County Durham. I was aged 16 when I left and the system, the institution where I had taken so many beatings, had formed the person I had become. I was released into a world that I didn't really know, and a world which didn't know me. Things were about to move forward quickly.

CHAPTER TEN

BORSTAL

AS I followed a screw into the governor's office at the borstal in West Yorkshire where I was doing time for a few robberies and muggings, I wondered what could be so important for the top man to ask to see me. But all was about to be revealed.

The screw knocked on the governor's door, was told to enter, and he positioned me standing in front of the main man's desk. Next to the Governor sat the priest attached to the borstal and a couple of other officers. I'd seen the priest before, but not at mass.

"John Cunningham?" The Governor asked.

"Yes," I said.

They all looked very serious and I remember thinking to myself what the hell have I done now to upset all this lot? The governor then took his spectacles from his eyes and looked up at me.

"I have some bad news for you, John," he said, and I was surprised because normally it was all surnames.

"John," he said, "I am very sorry to have to tell you that your father has died."

They all stared at me intently, obviously waiting for some kind of reaction from me. But I had no reaction to give them. They all looked perplexed. The governor then continued by saying that they had a procedure when an inmate loses a loved one. He said that I would be given two days compassionate leave to attend my father's funeral.

"I don't want to go anywhere," I said. "Let alone his funeral."

Without asking permission I then just turned and walked right out of his office. Who in their right mind if they had have taken time to find out about my history would think or presume that I wanted to mourn the passing of a father I never knew, cared for or had spent any time with?

In the years after getting away from the orphanage the only people I met and knew at that time were the people I had seen in the gloomy, smelly old pubs around Newcastle. At about that time I met up with one of the lads who was incarcerated with me in St Mary's Orphanage, none other than Harry Marsden. I had been working while I was at my 'mother's' house, where I ironically ended up after leaving the home. I was unemployed and the next thing I remember was Harry and I ending up mugging sailors and other people who were daft and careless enough to brag about what they had and how thick their wallets were.

We would just follow them, threaten them with violence and then take the money from them. Both Harry and I in the later years were not proud of that period in our lives, but at the time we couldn't live any other way. The inevitable happened and we were eventually caught and ironically I was sentenced to borstal, Harry on the other hand got three years in prison because he had already served a stint in borstal. I really can't remember much about borstal except that it was like a Labour Camp.

After a few months I certainly knew what Borstal was all about and it has often made me think, when I recalled the journey with the dour faced Catholic priest who delivered me to my 'mother', only for her to continue to abuse me. On reflection it would have been better for all the people we had mugged if, in the first place, the priest had just delivered me directly into the clutches of the borstal system.

It was during this period that I did something I was later to regret for my entire life, I was stupid enough to cover a lot of my body with tattoos. This was done with Indian ink and an ordinary needle. To be perfectly honest I have regretted this, especially the ones on my hands. One that I am happy with is the one that I put on my knee. It's an eye, you can be sure that with a third eye I did not miss a thing. I remained throughout my career very observant, and that tattoo always reminded me to make sure and keep them looking in the right direction.

Before my arrival in borstal at the age of fifteen I was told that I was being sent to a hostel in Newcastle and at the time I thought it was going to be an opportunity to escape the horrors that I had endured over so many years alone with nobody to help me over it or even the comfort of having a choice in the matter. When I arrived the feeling of joy and well-being faded immediately. It was a Catholic Hostel, another Catholic place, that I was so sure would continue to beat and flog me into total submission. The man that greeted me said that I had to call him the 'warden'. He was a truly miserable faced individual who relished in being a control freak. Not knowing what else I could do, I got into the daily routine of scrubbing and washing, of being kicked in the butt and generally verbally abused. Nothing had changed and I was still under the control of the local diocese. I got a job when I was there as an apprentice on a building site. After a year of this an incident took place that I will never forget, one that was in some way was a catalyst in sealing my future, one that I remember even to this day as if it was yesterday.

I had bought myself a jumper I liked on pay day. When I got back to the Hostel, the warden, who was a total fascist, told me to take it off. The 'warden's' name was Mr Taylor. I refused and looked him straight in the eyes, at which he completely lost his temper and he flew across the corridor at me.

Without thinking it through I went into a uncontrollable rage, nobody but nobody was going to take anything away from me again, my heart just raced at the time and when he went to grab me I just flew into him with a terrible anger and gave him a good battering. I used his own momentum and weight when he lunged at me and smashed his head into the wall; you know those old plaster walls with the wooden latts behind them? I just brayed the bastard's head all the way through. When I thought about it later I had just given him back a small piece of the floggings, beatings and abuse that I had endured over so many years. He received all the built up hatred and abuse that had been shown to me and, for me, this small incident was the last straw. They had taken every-thing from me over the years and now this man was treating me like a non person, he was truly a horrible man, it opened a whole can of worms for me. Where was this bloody Catholic God when we needed him? I know it just doesn't sound right, but I really enjoyed beating the shit out of this horrible man, but the reason I have told you this is because later in life I was to learn that this man Mr Taylor had fostered my sister Margaret and had treated her like dirt. Somehow a strange twist of fate had brought him here all these years later to me to be dealt with by being given a bloody good thrashing.

After this trick of fate and to what I can only now refer to as being 'Poetic Justice' to a man who was a complete hypocrite and in no way or circumstances could be referred to as man of any God – going to mass doesn't make one a better person than some-one else. I was immediately locked up and more or less denied any food or water until the matter had been dealt with. It was simple to them, but was in fact destined in the end to be the beginning of my career, one that I can truly say I enjoyed to the hilt. I was told that I was being sent to borstal. So there I was locked in a room at the hostel, my fate and future in the hands of these horrible people, who were not interested in why this event had taken place. Here I was at sixteen years old waiting to be shunted out to Borstal and I was very confused, and disturbed, and feeling by now extremely vulnerable. The worst of it was that I did not know what was going to happen to me. After two days of being locked in the room the door opened and a priest, a Father Gauhn, told me to get into his car.

Driving away from the hostel my mind started to play tricks on me wondering what kind of place borstal was, how would I be treated in this place, do we get beaten or thrown into a freezing bath? What was it like? I have to admit it was absolute fear I felt. I thought in retribution for what I had done to the warden I was going to suffer. I was like a frightened animal unable to move or to say anything. All the time during this journey the priest did not utter one word nor did he even glance at me sitting there, he just totally ignored me. I remember thinking at the time that this was part of the punishment I was going to receive at this place called borstal.

Eventually he stopped the car outside a house, I remember thinking to myself that this was a funny thing for a borstal to be, a normal everyday house! What was in there that was so important? Why stop here? Maybe he has to perform the last rights on somebody before we get there! Lot's of things just hit me like an avalanche and I was totally unprepared for the next part in this strange car journey. The priest gestured to me without a word to get out of the car. I remember his finger pointing to the door and an up and down gesture of his hand to go there. Still without a word he knocked on the door and we entered. Without looking at me he said this is your mother, so here I was after sixteen years being thrown back at the mercy of the very woman who had sealed my fate so many years earlier. The priest muttered something, but I didn't hear it and then left me with this woman. It was surreal. "Was this borstal?", I remember thinking to myself! So here I was back in the clutches of the woman who I had been taken away from for the reasons I have already explained. I didn't feel comfortable calling this woman 'mother' and I can still remember the shock and horror of that meeting to this day. It didn't take me long to realise that this woman was very violent and an extremely heavy drinker, as within hours she started to take me to what I now know to be horrible pubs. She paraded me round these pubs bragging to anyone that would listen that I was her son. I have nothing against these people, who were mainly prostitutes or people that most people in those days looked down on. I never looked down on them, far from it, to me they were just people down on their luck. Here I was then a vulnerable young boy who knew nothing about life in general being introduced and thrust into this environment. I promised myself then that I just wouldn't get myself into the same position again.

When she was drunk, I remember her telling everyone and me that she was proud of me. I just remember being totally confused and, in what I can now describe as shock, that I didn't really know this person. There was absolutely no bond, or any kind of love between me and this woman, and it wasn't long before we started to argue. She used to throw me out of the house and as a result I had to sleep in the garden, until I discovered a rusty old van which I started to use, simply because I had nowhere else to go. While I was at this strange woman's house my sister Margaret turned up out of the blue. I know, like me, Margaret was also in a state of shock. She also ended up arguing with this so called 'mother', who treated her as badly as she treated me. She constantly called Margaret a 'slut' and other dreadful things, but in reality Margaret only had one man in her life and that was her husband. This so called 'mother' would come in absolutely drunk at the end of the night and then throw everything at us, from the clock on the mantelpiece to anything else she could pick up. It was to us a new type of hell with the shouting and swearing making up every day life and the tension was unbearable.

One good thing to come out of that period of my life, and I do mean one thing, during the whole period that I stayed with this woman, was that I got a chance to meet up with my sister Maureen and two brothers who were lovely people. I often wonder how on earth they had survived what can only be termed as constant abuse over the years when I wasn't there. They had lived through nothing less than absolute chaos and the pressure of knowing that many times it was pointless going to bed as their mother would come in from the pub and cause absolute bedlam. My brother Michael had apparently been taken from St Mary's

Orphanage and Home some time before me to be returned to our 'mother'. I have since learned he was treated very badly by this woman who constantly called him every horrible thing you could imagine – he was treated like a slave – but more about Michael later. Luckily I didn't stay too long at 'mothers' and when she, yet again in a drunken rage, threw me out for the umpteenth time I ended up with my new address at Newcastle or should I say 'No fixed abode'. I just slept rough for a short time, but to me I was already a seasoned veteran having slept in the garden so many times. It was then that I teamed up with Harry Marsden and later ended up in borstal.

I remember just after leaving the orphanage I found myself in a shoe shop in Newcastle, and I picked up a shoe from the display and the assistant noticing that I was just staring at it asked if she could help me. I couldn't answer her, looking at it brought back memories of the *shoe-go-round* from the orphanage, where we would be given shoes to wear from the older 'prisoners' in the place – no trying them on for the right size – they made us wear them, even if they didn't fit, and even if they hurt like hell. I confess that poor assistant in the shop got the brunt of a lot of abuse when she simply asked: "Do you want to try them on Sir". If you are out there, sorry I didn't mean to lose my temper, it was just the shock of remembering this terrible time and the pain that it gave me for months, well until I got the next pair thrown at me that is.

I cannot remember exactly where I lived on my release from borstal, but it was shortly after my release that I ended up shacking up with a married woman, who was what they say 'on the game'. Contrary to what some people may think I was not solely dependant on her, in fact my criminal record will show that I was making money myself, which is why I served two prison sentences for thieving. During that time in my life I got to know a few women who were also 'on the game'. Looking back on it now it was nothing less than me being immature with a could-not-care-less attitude. I must admit that I found these women fascinating, however neither then nor now have I felt in any way proud of that time, but also, I don't feel ashamed of it. To me it was an eye opener and I indeed learned a great deal about sex then, which was, to be honest, all new to me. Being cooped up in St Mary's Orphanage, the Catholic Hostel, and then Borstal had seen to that.

This period of my life fortunately came to an end with no small thanks to a man called Davey Glover senior. One night I was overflowing with Brown Ale and some sort of tablets I had been given in the pub. I had a row with a couple of people, yet I was hardly able to stand and I was by now mortally drunk, however that strange instinct, whatever it may be, had got me back to where I was staying and I just crashed out on the bed. I had not locked the door and I heard a noise and the sound of someone talking and at that I opened my eyes and saw Davy standing there and despite being still drunk and half asleep I somehow jumped up off the bed and without thinking stupidly attempted to stick the nut on him. I was quite slim at that time and Davy was a very heavy man, I could hardly stand let alone fight anyone. God bless him though Davy, who could have taken a real liberty, to his credit just pushed me back onto the bed as I was attempting to hit him. I, of course, was completely incapable of doing anything anyway. Next thing I remember Davy had gone. I have always held Davy with respect for not taking a liberty, but at the same time there would have had to be serious consequences had he merely just done so.

After that incident I took stock of my situation and looked carefully at myself, probably for the first time in my life and I realised that I was going absolutely nowhere with my life as it was and it needed to be changed. Sometime before this incident I had applied to join the Merchant Navy. I really wanted to join, but I was refused because I had been to borstal. That was a real blow to me. As I saw it the system should have given me the chance to help me do the job that I would have liked to do, but it had put a black mark against me for life. To be perfectly honest it made me extremely bitter, as the only other choice for me was to get some menial job working for a mere pittance with no prospects. My thoughts then were why should I be doomed or sentenced to this kind of existence? It has to be remembered that I didn't get, or was ever offered, any kind of guidance or help by either society or from my so called parents. I ended up drifting into a life of crime, but this time it was professional crime and I took to it with a determination that I was going to be as good as one could get in my chosen profession.

CHAPTER ELEVEN

THE APPRENTICE

I learned how to use explosives in order to blow safes and by thunder I was a fast learner. I also learned how to knock out even the most sophisticated of alarm systems. As they say, practice makes perfect, and through dedication and hard work I was slowly but surely building up my reputation; to some criminals I was a pioneer for many things. I learned that I could send away for pamphlets and technical information on sophisticated alarms – you have to remember the very people who made them have also got to sell them – so I would pretend that I wanted to buy one. They readily sent me all the data I needed to learn how to beat them. As the word got out some of the big time criminals in the Geordie Mafia would seek me out for advice on this and that, or just to ask me how can I sort something out. They admitted that without my knowledge in many circumstances they would have had little success in some of the professional jobs that they were undertaking. They would know where there was a large sum of money, millions of cigarettes or maybe even a vehicle containing a large sum of money, they would then seek professional guidance. I have met people in the past who have not had professional guidance and have not bothered to get knowledge in order to do the 'Job' sweet as we would say. They would then run into a situation armed with some kind of weapon and when they got caught end up receiving an extremely long prison sentence.

In my time I was a very active villain and I also knew that by the law of averages I would get caught eventually, but what I can truly say is that I made millions during my career and yet I never saw the inside of a long term prison. I was once asked by a person in the media what my definition of a successful villain was. I replied that the whole object of the game is to make as much money as you can and do as little time in jail as you can.

The money, let alone the adventure and excitement, with a bonus of one up on the system, definitely outweighed the small sentences I served. I hardly had time to have a shave and then I was out again ready for the next rush. I believed in enjoying myself and in many ways I was simply making up for lost time; all that wasted time in St Mary's, the hostel and borstal was now being taken care off. I felt it was pointless saving it all up for old age only to realize and regret that they were then too old to enjoy it. Some of my good friends died at forty and after going to their funerals I realized even more that life is for the living and you are only young once so enjoy it. Some of my pals died young and left a lot of money behind and some of their money was gobbled up by vultures, so what a waste of effort that was.

Mario and Dave Courtney

Of course when a big 'Job' went down I would be one of the first on the suspect list, especially where any sophisticated alarms were rendered useless. Two safes were opened and cash and diamonds worth over £150,000 were taken. I knew right away that I would get a tug – 'questioned' – about it. As I suspected the police turned up and told me that a little dickey bird had told them that I was responsible for that job. I told them that my little dickey bird told me that it was in fact the police that were responsible and that it was all getting a bit confusing. They very reluctantly released me. It must be remembered that the hundred and fifty thousand pound job would in today's money be worth around a quarter of a million pounds, so it's hardly surprising that they had a dickey bird on the job.

By saying that I enjoyed my life of crime I realise that it will give some people reason to feel that I am a person with no conscience or shame, but if people were to have witnessed the despicable crimes that I have witnessed being committed and these by the very systems that we are supposed to respect, I am sure that they would come to a very different conclusion. By systems I don't just mean the brutality I suffered at the hands of so called caring people at St Mary's Orphanage and the Catholic Hostel, but those that I have witnessed committed by the police, prison warders, criminal and family courts, social services, the Army, sacred religious organizations and also the magistrates. I have even trapped Judges into admitting wrongdoing and also solicitors and many business people who pose as respectable members of the public. That is why I do not consider myself to be a bad person, if I were to be responsible for the extremely serious crimes that have been committed by the above named organisations, I truly would feel ashamed. In actual fact I know that I am incapable of committing such crimes as these real evil doers, who have lied, and trapped many in their webs of deceit.

Charlie Richardson, Harry Marsden, George Craig and Mario relaxing after a meeting.

One of the biggest injustices happened to a good friend of mine, Charlie Richardson, who I have met many times, mainly on his visits to North East England. It was 1966 when Charlie was on trial for five trumped-up counts of grievous bodily harm, with four others from a supposed torture gang, his brother Eddie, Tommy Clark, Frankie Fraser and Roy Hall. The so-called "Black Box" to give the alleged victims of the gang electric shocks did not actually exist. The inventor of this story was a police officer who, Charlie has always said, had a thorough grasp of the British psychology. He should have been in advertising or public relations. At the time, of course, it seemed Britain was in the grip of a mafia-style underworld, with the earlier activities of the Kray Twins making headline news and the memory of the Great Train Robbery, a few years earlier, still uppermost in the minds of the powers-that-be, particularly the judiciary. The trial of Charlie and his team was very much a political trial. The Establishment wanted to see him go down and go down heavily and, in what was a major travesty of justice, he was given a sentence which saw him serving 19 bloody years of his life for what in effect was nothing more than an alleged assault. Imagine that happening these days? You couldn't. If someone on an assault charge these days was given such a sentence there would be an outcry, claims of violations of that person's human rights and then as sure as night follows day there would be a huge, and winnable, claim for compensation.

What is little known about Charlie is that in 1966 police could not stop burglaries in South London but Charlie did. Knowledge is power but knowledge of power and how to control it became Charlie's hobby. What Charlie understood was the more a person trusts you, the more that person would do for you.

Tony Lambriano & Harry Marsden

A few years before the trial Charlie had had dealings with the Mafia in New York. The deal he had with them fell flat. It was not his fault but they were convinced he had cheated on them. They sent a man in a business suit round to his office to blow his head off with a revolver. Charlie was on his own in the office in London's Park Lane. The would-be hitman pulled out his gun, after getting confirmation of who he was, and started loading the chamber. Charlie wasn't going to plead for mercy or tell him how it was all a misunderstanding, he just legged it. He returned to the office later that afternoon and it was business as usual. He never saw the man again.

What Charlie's trial proved was that some supposed true criminals are prepared to stitch up any of their supposed friends if they in turn can benefit, by a lighter sentence for a crime they admit. This is absolute treachery of the highest order. In wartime if you give information to the enemy you are a traitor and would hang for it. Traitors in the criminal world who work with the enemy, ie the police, are given huge rewards, new identities and lifelong protection which costs the taxpayers millions of pounds. It's little wonder that knowing what I did about the corrupt criminal justice system and how supposed friends can become enemies that I worked alone most of my career. Charlie's antecedent history wasn't that of a big gang boss. He was only in his early thirties and on his way to becoming a millionaire when he went on trial. He had only ever been done for theft of a car, a book and six sides of bacon. All right, he had slapped a few low lifes around because they had broken the rules of the local community, but he was hardly British Mafia.

In the early 1960s, before Charlie's trial and when I was making a big name for myself in Newcastle and elsewhere, gaming machines in pubs and clubs were big business. Eddie and Frank Fraser were running a lucrative fruit machine business in clubs all over the West End of London. They did not need to use force, just persuade the owners to take their machines on a bigger percentage and get rid of the ones they had. Their empire grew and grew. They were offering the owners ten per cent extra and the kind of protection no one else could give them. Their influence began to expand much further than the West End, into the provinces and when a new club called Mr Smith and the Witchdoctor opened in Catford, Eddie and Frank were asked to install their machines. But a set of would-be gangsters led by the Hayward brothers, Billy and Flash Harry, who wanted to make a name for themselves in South London, started muscling in. There was a big carve up in Smith's club when the teams confronted each other and someone fired a sawn-off shotgun, hitting Eddie in the arse. Eddie and Frank ended up in hospital and were later arrested by police who were not on Charlie's payroll. Charlie had to step in to help but was otherwise distracted in South Africa, where he had legitimate mining interests. Ronnie Kray got wind of Charlie's problems in South Africa, and Eddie and Frankie's troubles, and had a brainwave. This was time for the Kray's expansion and only one person stood in his way – George Cornell, a trusted friend of the Richardsons. George had also called him a "fat poof" in public. While George sat with a friend in the Blind Beggar pub in Stepney Ronnie walked in and shot him in the face.

I mention that little bit of British criminal history because a murder happened in the North East linked to a fruit machine business later on the in 1960s which became major headlines and one of the men convicted of what was dubbed the first gangland killing in the region started his jail time in a cell next to mine in Durham Prison. But more on that later.

Security in the new unit within Durham Prison, a prison within a prison, for Category A prisoners, was built up after the escapes of train robbers Charlie Wilson and Ronnie Biggs from elsewhere. The Durham Maximum Security unit became the subject of an enquiry by Lord Mountbatten who said it had conditions "no civilized society could tolerate".

After serving 19 years of his 25-year sentence Charlie Richardson was finally released on August 24, 1984. That was more than a third of his life spent behind bars. What a flaming travesty!

CHAPTER TWELVE
MAKING A NAME

An incident involving a five-man team of dangerous Glaswegian men was what really bigged up my reputation in the underworld. I was by this time around twenty two years old and on a few occasions I had seen these men in and around the Bigg Market which is situated in the middle of Newcastle upon Tyne. They used to arrive out of the blue periodically and I must say they arrived in some style in a big black car aptly named a Humber Super Snipe. It was like something from an Al Capone film. They were indeed gangsters who had a reputation of leaving their mark on the faces of many people. They would sit in a bar in such a way that the lookers would see flashes of the extremely long and sharp razors which was their trade mark. This sight would in turn cause a ripple of fear to run through the veins of just about all of the hard men in Newcastle. On the night in question though I was in a pub called the Imperial, a pub which was always full of the top guys from the Newcastle underworld.

My girlfriend at the time was in a pub named the Chancellors which was on the other side of the Bigg Market. I remember I was chatting to one of the lads when I was then alerted by a friend of mine that my girlfriend had thrown a glass of beer into the face of one of the Glasgow mob during an argument. I instantly knew that there was trouble in the air and to be honest I was quite looking forward to it. I felt that it is always a better challenge when I was in combat with a known dangerous hard man, because for the winner in the underworld ratings I knew a defeat would not do me any good at all. The boss of the team was a notorious hell raiser named Jimmy Barr, a real Glaswegian name, he was up with the likes of the famous Jimmy Boyle.

There was a hushed atmosphere in the Imperial pub that night, a feeling of anticipation and I am not bragging when I say that I was as cool as one can be in such circumstances. Fear even at my young age was not in my vocabulary, my background had gotten rid of such emotions. I would do my very best then let fate decide the outcome, 'what will be will be', that was my motto. You could almost hear a pin drop as the pub door opened then all eyes in the place where fixed on the man entering. It was the boss himself, Jimmy Barr. He indicated for me to go outside with him with an air of total confidence. It must be understood that here was the man, he was also the man who was armed with a well used and trusted weapon, whereas I chose not to be armed at all. To get access to the saloon door itself one had to walk along an alleyway then do a right turn through one door, then after walking around three paces, one would enter the actual door leading into the room in which I sat. I had already figured out that his four henchmen could very well be waiting in the side alley and as I got up my eyes were fixed on his hands which were hanging down to be used obviously to draw out his razor.

We both were almost squeezed into the alcove between the two doors. It was there and then that he reached for his blade, almost instantly I hit him with a humdinger of a left hook which crashed into his nose and eyes at the same time my right hand tightly seized his lengthy curly hair, which enabled me with speed and force to guide his head onto my oncoming foot. I knew that after those two blows he was more or less fucked. However he some-how managed, maybe through fear, to throw himself at the door leading into the very room where all the boys were and they witnessed me finishing him off. I picked him up then grabbed his shirt collar just under his chin; I then gave him another left hook which sent him reeling through the hatch from which the barmaids served the drinks.

I ran through the hatch in order to give him one for the road, but he somehow found the strength to clamber up the optical, over the bar, then he fled through the door of the bar. It was then that I realised to my horror that he had dropped his bus pass and pension book (ha only joking). On returning back to my seat there was a lot of praise heaped upon me, which I gladly accepted. It was precisely at that moment I knew that I had without a shadow of any doubt earned the respect that a young lad of twenty two had been seeking from the age of fifteen. I had indeed found a home and the people of significance then became my adopted family. As for Jimmy Barr and his henchmen they were never ever seen in Newcastle again and many people were very relieved and happy to see the back of them.

An incident that arose that alerted the Geordie underworld that I was indeed a new kid on the block was a vicious altercation between myself and a well known danger man by the name of Clive Bates. The first time I met him was in Durham Prison when he was serving a lengthy Prison sentence for malicious wounding. He made a point of showing me the 'Court Evidence', which showed ferocious and deep wounds that he had inflicted on his victim. This was not a pleasant sight and I got the impression that he was making a point, one that I should really make a mental note of. For sure I did and decided that there was no way on earth I was ever going to trust him.

Clive Bates, or Clive 'Slasher' Bates as he was better known, was a very big thick set and strong bloke, by no means a pushover in anybody's book, but it puzzled me why a big bloke like him needed a weapon do the business. Win at all costs was obviously his motto, which is fair enough as long as he was disciplining his opponents for the right reasons. It was a case of three stripes and his victims were out, it was common knowledge that he carried his well used blade with him at all times. I know of many top hard villains who were shit scared of Clive and they could not be blamed for that, no one wants to be scarred for life do they.

I had arranged a meeting with Frank Dunbar who was a pal of Clive's. At this time both of them lived in the Chester-le-Street area of the North East, Frank asked me if it was ok for him to bring Clive through with him as Clive wanted to have a few drinks with me in Newcastle. To be honest against my better judgement I agreed. We met and had a few drinks in the Pilgrim's Club, up to that point Clive was on his best behaviour. We then went off to The Sun public house in Byker. Here we ended up in the company of Micky Hay and Alan 'The Fox' Martin. We were there for about an hour when Clive appeared to change, and he started to stare at the 'Fox' in a very menacing way. The 'Fox' had not given him any reason to be menaced in this way, it was obvious that something in Clive's mindset had caused him to want to inflict serious violence on someone.

He then made threatening remarks towards the Fox and by this stage the Fox was getting scared and would have fled the scene had I not indicated to him the best way I could to stay cool. I remember the music was loud and it was Abba singing Dancing Queen. The Fox was by now so scared you would think he was about to get torn apart by a pack of hounds as I did personally during the Jimmy Barr incident. I had my three eyes (the third is a tattoo on my knee) fixed on Clive's heavily tattooed hands. I also knew that violence was about to happen any second and honestly I was looking forward to it. It was a mixture of adrenalin and excitement. Remember violence was all that I had known from childhood, it was almost second nature to me, fear did not come into it. Clive, to the ordinary person, could and would frighten them with a look, he had the most menacing look and his eyes pierced through the very soul of his prey, and in this case it was the Fox.

There was a small table between Clive, the Fox and myself, but I was still able to keep my eyes fixed on Clive's hands. Sure enough within a flash Clive went for his weapon, at the exact same time my ringed fist crashed into his face knocking him clean off the stool he was sitting on. I was on to him hitting him with my fist, boot and with my head. He was indeed a strong bloke, but my onslaught on him was so fast and furious no hard man could have withstood it. When Clive was stretched out on the floor totally defeated and humiliated the Fox could not resist giving the now beaten man a kick in the head, shouting at Clive you will get more next time you bastard. We did find that amusing. Both Clive and poor Frankie Dunbar, who was innocent in all this, were then taken to the Central Station were I told Clive to never return again to Newcastle, with violence on his mind, or he would not get out alive next time.

I was told by a few people to be very careful because Clive had been known to jump from behind bushes to attack people; well I told them that he was welcome to try as he knew where I lived. A few months later I heard that Clive had changed his ways and was making himself a few quid, and then when I did meet him again it was good to see that he had changed for the better. I know for a fact that the change in Clive was due to that night in the Sun public house and to be honest I feel good about that.

In the early days I did quite a lot to bolster my reputation as a man to be reckoned with in the North of England. When I was in my early twenties I fought the hardest man in the town, Tommy Lamb, who was eventually stabbed to death. Tommy had a 100-strong team, all carrying razors, and they used to get into the Railway Canteen next to Newcastle Central Station. One day I was with my brother-in-law, Billy Dixon, and this fella came in and said Tommy Lamb wanted a word with me. He had just done six months for some kind of violence. I had basically been having a few rucks with some of his gang knocking them all out, and everyone had been hearing about me. He had no choice but to confront me because he was the main man in the town at the time. When we had a battle behind the Railway Canteen, which got split up by the Railway Police. We went round the back to have the fight. I knocked him down two or three times with a few good shots and then it started into a proper fight. It was a corker and I enjoyed it. I still have a small scar above my eye. Tommy was well beaten. Next thing we were getting parted by the police. Tommy Lamb then had total respect for me. We got cleaned up together in the Railway Station toilets and then he took me to his home where we had something to eat and a couple of drinks.

There was another big name in Newcastle who I had a run in with in the early days. His name was Harry Perry. One night in Billy Botto's club in Byker I was dancing on the dance floor. There was a gang from Longbenton and this one who wanted to make a name for himself deliberately pushed my woman so I bided my time a while and when he came back I gave him three or four belts and he went flying across the polished floor on his arse, ending up at the feet of Harry Perry. Harry, who was a minder in there, said "you fucker", and I said "Harry, get rid of that fella".

Another time I was with my mate Harry Marsden who had been accused of something and there was no evidence. I told Harry Marsden he had to take it seriously. I told him we needed to go down to the lion's den and face the accusers. I told him if he didn't do it then it would spread round like a cancer and it would stick with him the rest of his life. So we went into Billy Botto's club, sat down, people were dancing, and then Harry Perry comes in and Paul Tucker, who was a boxer, big Ernie Wright and two or three others. Paul Tucker didn't know Harry Marsden. After about 15 minutes or 20 minutes of glares and tension I asked Paul to come over. I introduced him to Harry Marsden and told him we knew what he was accused of but I see no evidence that he did that and for that reason I'm with him. I said if there's going to be trouble here there will be certain people at the end lying on the dance floor and it won't be us. He paused for a while and then he said he hadn't really spoken in depth to the accuser, who was known to him. After that nothing more was said about it and Harry Marsden's reputation was intact.

On another occasion I was drinking with Marky Kelly in the Three Bulls and I told him I was going down to the Half Moon Inn because there was going to be a spot of bother. A lad called Geordie (and theres many of them in Newcastle), who was a boxer and big fella, was there with Jimmy Gardner and a few other local faces. Geordie came over and asked if I had done something which had upset him. I said yes I did. I got him to the floor and rammed his head about ten times, until he was weakened. They actually made a ring around where we were fighting. Then Geordie went round Elswick in Newcastle shouting "Mario's Took Me Crown". Later one of Geordie's relations shot Harry Perry in the groin and got six years for it.

Well, in the mid seventies I was on the verge of retiring from crime, in fact I was actually working for a building firm, yes it was legal, but unfortunately I sustained a serious head injury which caused brain damage and this injury also brought on a condition called ME. ME causes chronic fatigue with constant headaches. To make matters worse it caused a cyst on the brain which in turn caused further brain damage, causing me to loose the quality of life I had by now grown used to. I am now forced to spend much of my time lying in bed or between fleeting periods of not feeling bad trying to get on with whatever life that I am able to grab between the periods of exceptional pain. I was actually in Newcastle General Hospital waiting to have a brain operation, only to discover that the doctors at the last minute decided it was just too dangerous to operate on, leaving me with no hope and having to bear up to the problem and the pain I have to endure. When I questioned this, the doctors said that the operation was too dangerous and would probably mean that I would be at an extremely high risk of losing the use of my limbs and that I would just have to learn to live with the condition as best I could. I told the doctors that I was prepared to take the risk and have the operation and that if it did fail and I lost the use of my limbs that I would make sure that they all got a good pair of expensive shoes out of it as they wouldn't be any use to me then. Well they just laughed. In fact the only good thing that came out of it was I did actually see my brain and I pity those that only think they have one.

After the injury I was unable to work, which left me with no other choice than to rely on state handouts or, as they call it, incapacity benefit. This they assured me would provide me with a decent standard of living. Well as you can imagine £40 does not go very far and if they call this a decent standard of living I sure as hell would not want to be invited to their houses for Sunday dinner. I felt as though I was again being penalised for having the misfortune to have a chronic medical condition. My quality of life was nil. I felt as though I was being thrown on the scrap heap. No one in the system cared a fuck, their answer was deal with it and get on with it. There was absolutely no way I was going to live the rest of my days living on the breadline, so despite my medical condition I had to pace myself and that was on the odd occasion that is when I had enough strength and focus. I would lie in the back of the car with my medication to go away and do a 'job' or crime in order to supplement the meagre Giro that I was expected to survive on.

One of the jobs we had to abandon, which had taken a lot of planning, was a job in Glasgow. When our convoy of two cars was travelling through Scotland we saw fire in the sky and then later thought we were being followed by police. We had actually driven into the aftermath of the Lockerbie Air Disaster when Pan Am Flight 103 exploded in mid air over the Scottish village, killing 180 people. We abandoned the planned job and returned home in a sombre and thoughtful mood.

There was a time, in the 1970s, when Maggie Thatcher was telling people that they had to put up with a financially hard period due to high inflation. Yes, I could understand that, but the trouble was that whilst I was expected to live on poverty money, she and her pals were receiving large salaries, eating and drinking in the Houses of Parliament Bar and buggering off on nice holidays to exotic locations. They all had nice big houses, servants, posh cars and money in the bank. It finally came to the crunch when Maggie Thatcher told the nation that what this country needed was more entrepreneurs! Well here I am Maggie, I am waiting in the wings. It then occurred to me that I should put my skills to some use, serve my country and do some good for myself to boot.

If Maggie and her henchmen, that is all those with the big fat salaries, had proved to me that they could live on £40 a week then that would have been different. I would quite happily have joined them. But as far as I was concerned they did not lead by example. "I'm alright Mario", was their motto, but luckily I had the courage and bottle to get out (when possible) to earn money, in my own way, despite the risk of years in prison. So thank you Maggie you were right, entrepreneurs do work hard, those safes are after all very heavy! I might not have been as fit or focused as I used to be in my prime, but my country needed me and I was certainly not going to let the side down. I still played my part. Some of the lads I worked with used to tell me that I must have a heart like a lion, because by then I was over fifty years in age and suffering from a chronic illness.

They say that violence begets violence. After being on many occasions myself the victim of violence and after witnessing serious violence throughout the whole of my childhood it now comes as no surprise that I have inherited this trait. Anyone who knows me from my teenage years and now will tell you that I literrally fought my way to the top of becoming one of the top guns in the crime world, or the Geordie Mafia as it's referred to now. Violence was almost second nature to me and yet I feel confident in saying that I have not been a bully.

I have not and never will be a liberty taker, in fact people who know me will tell you that I was and am the absolute opposite to what a bully is perceived to be, in effect I have my self been bullied by the bullies in the orhpanage. I have also fought and beaten men twice my size. I have fought and beaten men who were armed with weapons including a couple of men with a gun, the gun which I would, after beating them up, threaten to stick it up their arse. It is no good having a gun if the carrier of the weapon has not got the nerve to use it. It may sound stupid and reckless to attack someone who is standing in front of you with a weapon of some kind, but for some reason it did not deter me in the slightest.

The only explanation I can give for this mind set is that I must obviously be a fatalist, with the mind in a 'whatever will happen will happen' mode – what will be will be. I am indeed a fatalist. I then wonder why most of the other people, who I shared my childhood with, are not like me. In fact some of them are the exact opposite, their childhood experiences crushed them both emotionally and physically, which sadly is probably why some of them committed suicide or became serious alcoholics, or lived their lives alone like hermits such as Brian Marsden. Brian was so emotionally damaged by his childhood spent within the confines of St Mary's Orphanage that he still has terrible nightmares and is as a consequence rarely ever seen outside his house.

I feel that the reason for the big difference between men like Brian and myself is that we are all different. I have been extremely lucky enough to survive. I must have been given the strength to stay strong to fight and battle my way through life. I have had the tools within my make up to survive, where the less fortunate ex orphanage boys 'went under' due to the damage bestowed upon them as children. Looking back I realise that I was an extremely angry young boy when I left St Mary's, which showed itself when I thrashed that religious bigot warden Taylor in the hostel. I was just seventeen years of age then, and I have never shown any fear of anyone no matter how big they are or what their reputation may be. If any one challenged me they got a good licking but not with my tongue. I can understand why just about everyone does not exactly like the thought of death, I am not exactly looking forward to it either, but death is inevitable, it comes to everyone and it is in the human psyche to want to cling to life. However, it is final, and when we look into life itself, and when we think of time, we are only on this planet for a fleeting moment.

When thinking of eternity, in a thousand years time it will be as though we had never existed, such is the mystery of life. Above all dying is beyond our control and that's what makes it so difficult for most people to accept. Life is too precious to us, which is why it is natural for us to want to hang on to it for as long as possible. I am not sure whether fear is the right word regarding the thoughts of ones death, but it may be because death itself is completely out of our control.

Big business, yes well I have spoken to big business people and they have admitted to me that they employ the young as they only have to pay the minimum wage or less. If they can get away with it and yes they have admitted to me that if they want more for the pittance they are being paid, they merely finish them and get another. Why is it not surprising that a lot of young people are losing faith in the system when they are merely being used in this way. It's not surprising then that they realize what is happening and then turn to crime? Some though get some support, they are the lucky ones, but the one's who can't get any kind of support have no other choice than to turn to crime or drugs, which means more crime to finance their habits.

There is no quality of life if you cannot afford it. Most youngsters are left with no choice, if they want to keep up with fashion, or merely be able to afford to go out, they need to find money to support it. It's not surprising that the rate of suicides is on the increase amongst young people when you consider this, so many of them just give up on a society that has in effect abandoned them.

It's hardly surprising if it's like that now. You can bet it was a lot worse through the 60's, 70's, 80's and in to the early 90's and that in a nutshell is why I went on to become a founding member of what they now call the Geordie Mafia. When we talk about this you have to remember that it was a case of sticking together, looking after one another. I had never known a real family life and here I was with a family that would quite literally die for me and me for them, make no doubt about it. Many families aren't that close even today and it's hard to put into words what that meant for me. All the years that had passed, by that time, had in effect prepared me, or moulded me, into what I was now to become. People say 'give respect – earn respect'. I had finally and inevitably found that with guys who were at that time in the same situation as me. We didn't really have a chance, as it was preordained what was about to happen was thrust on us by the very system that tried to stifle us. We wanted some of the money that the rich and corrupt were enjoying and we sure as hell were going to get it. The difference though was that we didn't want to hurt anyone in the process. As you read on you will see that there were some funny sides to it and it's understandable why such a lot of the old aged pensioners, or have nots around at that time, referred to me as 'Robin Hood'.

As you will learn from the chapters to follow and the police evidence presented to the courts, we only ever kept the cash from the safes we acquired, many of the other items we distributed round the needy in Newcastle. This was what we thought was poetic justice for all the hurt and corruption that had been hurled at all of us in the past, by Government and society in general. I can still dearly remember one old aged pensioner's absolute delight when we gave him a pile of TV Stamps and several bags of loose change, to me that made it all worthwhile. It was the simple things that we got out of it that made all the difference. Sure as hell the 'Robin Dude' had arrived to wreak havoc round Scotland and England. Nowhere was 'SAFE', pardon the pun, if it had a safe, never mind the security 'compliments of the post office'. With a bit of careful planning it could be done.

CHAPTER THIRTEEN
LAST MAN HANGED

On the morning of the last execution in Durham Prison there was a deathly silence and I learned later that many of the prisoners had not slept well at all, they were impeded from their sleep by the thoughts of what was about to happen. A man was going to die almost right under their own feet, you can be sure that I also did not sleep very well that night. Next morning when the jailers came on duty they did not open up the cells for the inmates to go for breakfast which is the normal morning routine. Every single inmate remained locked up. The silence was almost deafening, it was indeed a very strange and weird atmosphere and 9am was the time that the doomed man was due to die. Shortly before 9am the condemned man would be given the breakfast of his choice, he would then be seen by the chaplain, ironically a man whose God is renowned for his forgiveness. But this man of God who knows that, no matter what his personal views, he is participating in the 'killing' of another human being. He probably feels that he must go with the flow and do what he is told. So much for that chaplain's morality, although he is a small cog within a big wheel known simply as the legal system, he surely knew that he was taking part in a premeditated killing, but he is like most people, too weak, lacking the courage of his own convictions, he is a follower, weak people who 'just go with the flow' are a big factor as to how and why injustices occur.

At the stroke of 9am the trap door opened up and this misguided young man died dancing his final dance with what had become, by this time, a broken neck, hanging there like a piece of meat in a butcher's shop. It was at that moment that all the pent up tension exploded into an uproar as all the inmates started to bang on the steel cell doors of their cells with whatever they could get there hands on. There was shouting and some inmates actually wept. The sounds must have been heard by most people in Durham. The racket continued for some time until the inmates had released all of the built up tension that had been building up in the days before the hanging. Then, just as suddenly as it started, there was silence. It was indeed a weird and totally emotional outburst. For me it just reinforced my belief that human beings indeed act in a cruel and revengeful way, and this in such an organised and premeditated way. The state would kill other human beings in our name, which in effect makes us all killers. Because the biggest factor of the lot is 'human nature', this against the laws of averages dictates without doubt that sooner or later, an innocent person or persons would die, because there is nothing perfect about human beings and human nature, there certainly is not one country in the whole world which can honestly say that it has a perfect legal system.

The death penalty was finally and, in my view correctly, abolished in 1964. Before this my mate Johnny Bolem, his brother Tommy and myself were crammed into the same cell, a cell which was approximately twelve foot by six foot. We were there when the execution of the last man to hang in Durham Prison took place. I can remember his home address was in Teesside, or as it is now known, Cleveland. The exact date escapes me but my memory of that day has stayed with me to this day. I can recall the few days building up to the unfortunate guy's execution, there was nothing less than a real tension pervading the whole prison and you could almost feel this surreal and weird atmosphere. Every prisoner could not help but feeling almost as if he was an integral part of the execution of this man, which as it worked out was to take place right under our cell. We would quietly talk about, and try to understand what must be going on in the mind of the doomed young man who was in effect 'waiting' or preparing himself to die.

We would think of the family of the condemned man and how it must have felt for them knowing that in effect a strange person or persons were waiting in the wings to kill a member of their family. Their own loved one, their own flesh and blood. We would also think and talk about the family of the victim who had also lost a loved one and who would now be seeing this tragic scenario unfolding in a completely different way to that of the condemned man's family; two families trapped in this horrific situation. I have already said that my opinion of life is that a large percentage of our lives are simply dictated by 'fate and circumstance', which indeed is beyond, or out of, our control. In effect the destiny in regards to what was about to take place and the drama of what was unfolding was now only in the tarnished hands of the state, to hang the man was what it was all about.

I came to my decision that it was right to abolish the death penalty not only because we now know that innocent people have been executed, and that many more would have or could have been executed, for example the Birmingham six and the Guildford four. These people would without doubt all be dead by now, executed by the state. Miscarriage of justice is misleading terminology because it suggests that cases like the above mentioned were just some kind of tragic 'mistake'. These were not mistakes though, these people were convicted because of downright lies and police corruption. Unjust and wicked tactics were used to force them to confess to a very serious crime which they did not commit, and the arrested people who did not make a statement of confession discovered later that the police made up the statement for them. When it was eventually 'proved' that the case was what we call a 'pure stitch up' it was too late for the innocent people who had by this time served 16 years in prison. In fact one of them paid the ultimate price and died in prison. You may ask what happened to the corrupt people within the system that engineered this situation? Well, as per usual in these cases, 'nothing'. Where was the state's justice when the perpetrators of this terrible crime were not punished for what they did. They should have received a life sentence for such a horrific crime against those innocent people, and the tears and heartache it had caused for their families over the years.

People who argue for a return of the death penalty say that with the now available evidence obtained from DNA and the tape recordings made during police interviews, it would be very unlikely to convict an innocent person. I wonder if the pro-death penalty people are aware that almost anyone could place their DNA at the scene of a serious crime, including murder. It would only take some clever investigator to mess up the arrested person's 'alibi' for instance. Such evidence then gets put to a jury and the innocent person could very well get convicted resulting in the death penalty. In my time I have found and met many adults who have the mental age of a child. They could quite easily or inadvertently say something during interrogation which then incriminates them; we have all of us become aware of such cases. I could go on and on quoting cases, of wrongful convictions, and believe me their are many wrongful convictions despite "infallible" DNA evidence.

The pro-death penalty brigade should seriously consider how they would feel if it was one of their own loved ones who ended up dancing from the end of a rope, then later to be proved to be an innocent person. People should think very long and deeply before they comment on such serious subjects. Remember, unfortunately I was in a position that enabled me to observe and study just about all of these large and so called righteous institutions. Sadly, I have been a victim of most of them. I really do know at first hand what I am talking about. I believe that hanging people until they are dead is wrong and when it is done by the state it is no less than a premeditated killing of another human being who may or may not be guilty. Where there is even the remotest possibility that innocent people could die in such a barbaric and unjust way, and no matter what so called safety measures are put into place, it will never be safe, the death penalty can never be justified.

One of the most serious miscarriages of justice, of which there were many, was of course that of Derek Bentley, hanged for a crime he didn't commit. On the night of 2 November 1952, Chris Craig and Bentley tried to break into the warehouse of a confectionery manufacturers and wholesalers in Croydon. The two youths were spotted climbing over the gate and up a drain pipe to the roof of the warehouse by a young girl in a house across the road from the building. She alerted her parents, and her father called the police.

When the police arrived, one of them, Detective Sergeant Frederick Fairfax, climbed the drain pipe onto the roof and grabbed hold of Bentley. Bentley broke free and was alleged by a number of police witnesses to have shouted the words "Let him have it, Chris". Both Craig and Bentley denied that those words were spoken.

Craig, who was armed with a revolver, opened fire, grazing Fairfax's shoulder. Fairfax arrested Bentley. Following the arrival of uniformed officers, a group was sent onto the roof. The first to reach the roof was Police Constable Sidney Miles, who was immediately killed by a shot to the head. After exhausting his ammunition and being cornered, Craig jumped some thirty feet from the roof, fracturing his spine and left wrist when he landed on a greenhouse. At this point, he was arrested.

Craig would not have faced execution if found guilty, as he was below the age of 18 when PC Miles was shot. Bentley on the other hand was not. The trial took place before the Lord Chief Justice of England and Wales, Lord Goddard, at the Old Bailey in London between 9 December 1952 and 11 December 1952. The doctrine of 'constructive malice' meant that a charge of manslaughter was not an option, as the 'malicious intent' of the armed robbery was transferred to the shooting. Bentley's best defence was that he was effectively under arrest when PC Miles was killed; however, this was only after an attempt to escape, during which a police officer had been wounded.

As the trial progressed the jury had more details to consider. The main question was what Bentley had meant by "Let him have it", if indeed he had said it, which he claimed he did not. If he had said it he could have meant "shoot" or, alternatively, he might have been telling Craig to surrender the gun.

Bentley was illiterate and of low intelligence, almost considered retarded, but was also considered sane, fit to plead and to stand trial. The jury took 75 minutes to decide that both Bentley and Craig were guilty of PC Miles's murder. Bentley was sentenced to death with a plea for mercy on 11 December 1952, while Craig was ordered to be detained at Her Majesty's Pleasure. He was released in 1963 after serving 10 years' jail.

Bentley's lawyers filed appeals but failed in their efforts and he was hanged at Wandsworth Prison at 9am on the morning of 28 January 1953. On 30 July 1998, the Court of Appeal set aside Bentley's conviction for murder 45 years earlier.

Though Bentley had not been accused of attacking any of the police officers being shot at by Craig, for him to be convicted of murder as an accessory in what is known as a joint enterprise it had to be proven that Bentley knew Craig was armed and that he had not withdrawn from the "joint enterprise". He must have withdrawn as he was under arrest at the time. Another element in his defence was that a 'confession' by Bentley said to have been recorded word for word, had been heavily edited by police officers.

There was a case in the North East of England which I followed with interest which had some similarities to that of the Bentley and Craig case. In July, 1997, in a House of Lords judgement, Philip English, from Tyneside, was cleared of murdering Sergeant Bill Forth in March 1993 in Gateshead. English had been hand-cuffed before his friend Paul Weddle killed Sgt Forth with a concealed knife. The existing 'joint enterprise' law allowed the conviction of English for murder because they had both been attacking Sgt Forth with wooden staves, making English an accessory to any murder committed by Weddle as part of that assault. Law Lords made the 'fine distinction' that a concealed knife was a far more deadly weapon than a wooden stave, so that proof of English's knowledge of it was necessary for conviction. It is said that that appeal may have influenced the allowing of a posthumous referral of the Bentley case.

The Bentley case, resulting in the death penalty for an innocent man, may have been one of the most high-profile miscarriages of justice in this country, but how many other people are now languishing in jail when their convictions are either unsafe or they have been fitted up? I couldn't hazard a guess, but I imagine there will be quite a few.

The biggest criminals, who get little or no attention from the bizzies, are, of course, what they call white-collar criminals, those pen-pushers who work for private companies and defraud their firms to line their own pockets or, even worse, those who work for public organisations, such as local councils or the government, who steal the money of the tax-paying public. The biggest frauds ever perpetrated by these middle-class villains who hide behind a veneer of respectability have, of course, happened on the financial markets, but very, very few of them have ever been brought to justice. The vast majority of white-collar criminals, who have fleeced more people out of many more millions than have the collective efforts of professional villains like me, have got away scot free with most of their crimes. The odd conviction has happened, to perhaps assuage the genuine complaints of injustice by a public who are not as unintelligent as the authorities would like us to believe.

Mario in the 70s

As I was making a name for myself on the crime career front in Newcastle in the 1960s and 1970s one such case surfaced which brought down the Leader of Newcastle City Council. Some people referred to him as 'Mr Newcastle', others as 'The Mouth of the Tyne', but his real name was Thomas Daniel Smith, which he later shortened to T Dan Smith, using the first initial of his first name because of an embarrassing incident at Newcastle Airport involving another man called Dan Smith.

T Dan Smith led the city council from 1960 to 1965 and was a prominent figure in the Labour Party in the North East of England. He was also as bent as a nine bob note. Smith formed business links with architect John Poulson which led to his trial for accepting bribes in April 1974, at which he pleaded guilty and was sentenced to six years' jail. Smith, the son of a miner, was born in Wallsend, near Newcastle. He was politically influenced by both his parents who held strong left-wing views. He was unemployed during the 1930s but founded his own painting and decorating business in 1937 which was known for being very sparing in the amount of paint it used (its local nickname was 'One-Coat Smith'). He became a member of the Labour Party in 1945 and in 1950 he was elected as a councillor in Newcastle and became Chairman of the city's Labour Group in 1953.

When the Labour Party won the 1958 local elections and took control of Newcastle, Smith was appointed Chairman of the Housing Committee. His success in launching new housing schemes led to his promotion to Leader of the Council in 1960. As Leader he gave positions of power to his political allies and friends, excluded members of all other parties, and made sure those Labour Party members who disagreed with him were never given any influence. It was a very similar set up to that what most councils have today; all the key money decisions being made by a clique or inner circle who all have vested interests in towing the line. Who said power corrupts and absolute power corrupts absolutely? Smith was, physically, quite an intimidating man and he had a loud voice.

Smith pushed ahead with his plans to clear Newcastle of slum housing, including some of the tenement blocks where I used to live in the West End, and regenerate the city, which which would have been all very honourable if it hadn't involved corruption.

101

Smith began linking his political ambition with his personal greed and his desire for personal wealth, and this became his downfall. His own painting and decorating business received more than half of the contracts for council housing in the city, something that did not go unnoticed. In 1962 he started a public relations firm to support redevelopment of other areas in the region, and later nationwide and with this firm he formed links with John Poulson, an architect who was hungry for business and was known for paying those who could supply it, probably in brown paper envelopes. Smith eventually received £156,000 from Poulson for his work, which typically involved signing up local councillors on to the payroll of his companies and getting them to push their councils to accept Poulson's development schemes. Poulson earned more than £1million through Smith. Poulson acted as architect for many prominent buildings in the North East and beyond, including the new Gill Bridge Avenue Police Station which was built in Sunderland, ten miles from Newcastle.

Smith was a friend and ally of North East Labour stalwart Andy Cunningham, who was also brought down by the Poulson scandal and served a jail sentence.

Smith's PR firm was involved with Wandsworth Borough Council in pushing a redevelopment scheme, where its contact was Alderman Sidney Sporle. Sporle fell under police suspicion of corruption in the late 1960s and an inquiry led to Smith being charged with bribery in January 1970. Although acquitted at trial in July 1971, Smith was forced to resign all his political offices. Subsequently, Poulson's 1972 bankruptcy hearings disclosed extensive bribery and in October 1973 Smith was again arrested on corruption charges. He pleaded guilty in 1974 and was sentenced to six years' imprisonment; despite his plea he continued to assert his innocence.

T Dan Smith was probably one of the most talented and cunning villains in the North East. Take away his power in the council, his expensive clothing, and his links with influential big wigs, he could have ended up as the Geordie Godfather, taking over from me. In a way he was the Godfather of Newcastle, but he got too greedy and with too much greed comes sloppiness, as all villains know. Smith was not averse to dealing with underworld figures and in fact was once paid a substantial sum in a brown envelope by the one armed bandit tycoon Vince Landa to ensure a planning application for car parking spaces near the Dolce Vita nightclub was passed without any problems.

Most villains do not have any other income than crime, so they can't hide behind the facade of doing business, like the T Dan Smith's of this world. But how many of these respectable people are on the fiddle, from defrauding their own firms to fiddling their own expenses? Probably hundreds of thousands who will never get their white collars felt. That's another injustice which makes me angry.

CHAPTER FOURTEEN

PATCHES

WHEN I was eventually banged up again in Durham Prison the screws and governors were all delighted to see me. I was given a VIP reception and I remember thinking at the time that I should have bought a bus pass, just in case. They had prepared the VIP suite for my arrival and as soon as they had searched me and dusted me down they placed me on 'Special Watch'. I thought it must be my good looks. They obviously were well prepared for my return, they had even managed in the short time before my arrival to organize a nice new uniform. Gone was the plain grey uniform, they gave me one with bright yellow stripes. Well I asked what it was all about, it was a nice suit but it made me look like a death's head caterpillar. They told me that it was a new uniform for escapees so that we would stand out. They said I should feel honoured as I was the very first prisoner to be issued with one.

The screws were more interested in asking me questions about the escape. They wanted to know how I had managed in such a short time to evade capture and more importantly how I was able to slip through the security net, which they had wrapped around Durham City. I told them nothing and it was obvious that they wanted to know so that they could stop anyone else from doing the same again. Well it was only a matter of time before the inevitable happened. The two screws who were on duty the night I escaped and fled from Durham were again on duty on the landing that I was on. As I was an at risk from escaping I had to fold my clothes every night and place them on a chair that was then put outside my cell door each night. The pair of them tried a few tricks on me to make my life harder and more difficult for me. It was obvious that they had a grudge as I sure as hell didn't help their promotion prospects. It was just their revenge for me making them look like idiots. One lunch time I was sitting on my bed when one of them came in to give me my mail. I didn't get off the bed, so he had to come right in to the cell. As soon as he got near enough to me I jumped up and slid the bolt into a position were the door wouldn't be able to lock. I dragged the screw into the corner of the cell and immediately he started to crap himself. He was in fear of his life, but it happened so quickly he didn't get a chance to utter a word. I pinned him up against the cell wall and told him that if he tried any more silly business with me he would be in serious trouble and that no governor or system would be able to help him. It must have dawned on him in those brief seconds that I meant what I said, "don't fuck with me anymore or I will get you someday, somehow". I then flung him out of the cell. On that he could have reported me to the governor, or he could have pressed the panic button, but he obviously realised that I could also have had him sorted by one of my contacts or that I would get him in the near future. Well needless to say I had no more bother from either of them again and if anything they were more polite when saying anything to me. What they didn't know was that we already had enough good intelligence on them to have them sorted on the outside if there was any bother, although I am sure they already knew that.

Mario in a cell at HMP Acklington.

But it wasn't just the screws who would give you grief. There was also the odd other prisoner who would want to have a go to boost their own reputations. One day I felt a sharp blow to my head. I just coolly turned round grabbed the man and then I lost it completely. Seeing red I put my hands around his big fat neck and started to seriously strangle him. I remember his face going blue and by this time his feet were off the ground, fortunately for the big shit some of the other inmates pulled me off him shouting "Mario he's not worth it." They just kept telling me he's not worth getting a murder stretch for and eventually I calmed down. That big bully, when he recovered, pleaded with the screws to be put on rule 43 for his own protection.

I don't really know why, but for some strange reason I don't fear anyone, it's probably all the abuse I had when I was younger on top of all the horrible things I had seen in Mosside and Liverpool, but it's the way I have had to deal with life. I just don't care how hard they are, what their reputation is, who they know or even how big they are, hurt me and expect to get more in return is my motto. It soon became apparent that my reputation was growing and in a way I began to get a lot of respect, that word means a million dollars to you outside, but inside it can save your life. Quite simply by attacking the bullyboys the other inmates began to respect me as someone who would not merely sit back and accept their crap. The bullyboys would spread fear and expect everyone to bend to their rules, they didn't get away with it with me and I felt a sense of pride in that. I am obviously a fatalist. I once fought a black guy in Leeds Prison. He would boast to everyone that he had a black belt in Judo, but I done him in a matter of seconds, much to my surprise I have also given a good hiding to a few boxers as well and come out of it in one piece.

A thank you from the screws, well what's that all about you may wonder? Well again it was due to yet another bullyboy who ruled his little domain in Liverpool Prison with a rod of iron. He had prior to my arrival severely hurt a lot of people in there. It was truly a good thing that I ended up there, as you can remember I had enjoyed my time previously in Liverpool when I was on holiday from Durham Prison. I had just arrived and I was no sooner in the cell when the door opened and this big shit said to me, look you need to pay your way in here to survive, what do you have? I said I have a good left hand that's going to meet up with your nut in the next few minutes, at that he laughed and I remember thinking shit here we go again, no rest for the wicked. I jumped on him as I very systematically gave him a bloody good hiding, truly I was really enjoying it, although from the look in his by now red eyes, he didn't appear to be enjoying it as much as I was. Next thing I knew was the screws pulling me off him and in the background everyone shouting give him some more, he sure would have got a lot more, but for the intervention of the screws. That's it I thought make an entrance and get solitary for your first week, but that didn't happen. They dragged him away and a screw from the safety of the door said don't worry son, you've just made our lives a lot better. I looked at him and he went on to say that the guy I had just pulverised was nothing less than the prison bully, giving the screws as much as he gave to the other inmates and it was about time somebody faced up to him. I was shocked: there I was giving this Tyson look alike or shithead a hiding and getting thanked for it by the screws! Well I ask what's the chances of that happening. I turned and told the screw to fuck off and that I beat him up for me not them, the screw just looked at me, but I could see in his expression that he knew to keep away from me.

Everyone needs to understand that prison has it's own rules and it's own way of handling things. The strict regime that exists there and the prison's own rules have embedded in them another set of rules put into place, governed and executed by the inmates themselves. This all follows to the letter a strict code of etiquette and unwritten laws that govern an inmate's behaviour with his fellow inmates or between the inmates and the screws who are really only there to make your time inside quite simply as unpleasant as possible.

You have to understand that in prison you have to have principles. It's a different kind of life and all the years of incarceration when I was a child taught me this. If anyone tried to challenge me or tried to pull a stroke on me, they quite simply had to be seriously punished if only to warn anyone else that if they messed with me inside that's what they could expect in return. It was fortunate for them that this didn't have to happen too often and it was rarely the case that I had to do anything. However, I have been in a few prisons were the bullyboys ruled the roost, they rarely even looked at me, but if they started to give me the once over I would immediately attack them and give them a good going over: a good thrashing works wonders. This often happened much to the delight of the inmates who were at that time suffering at their hands and being bullied by them. I came to believe that if you went to a strange prison, you have to let the inmates there know that you were not a person to be messed around with. When you live in a jungle it's only the strongest that survive. In prison nothing else matters than surviving your term of incarceration, you have to get respect, or you may not come out of the other side. In one prison a bullyboy attempted to get revenge on the thrashing I had given him by sneaking up behind me with a blade and slashing me on the back of the head. He paid the price with a severe good hiding.

In the early days in prison I organised with some of the other inmates a few riots, well it broke up the monotony for one thing, and it was often the only way we could get the screws to listen. On one particular occasion we heard that some of the screws were abusing another inmate, so we brought the whole prison to a halt. We would throw everything from bricks to slates, smashing up as much as we could get our hands on. It is often the case that the only way you can make a change is to fight for it. The system hated it when we kicked off. Prison in those days was harder than it is now. We had no television and no radios either, there were three inmates to a small cell and the stench in prison is a smell of its own, one you never forget.

Prison can often be an 'unreal' place. For instance I went into one cell to have a bit of a crack (talk) with two of the lads, then one of the lads began to write a letter and I started reading one of his magazines. After a few minutes I looked up from the magazine and the other cell mate was against the door standing on his head, saying nothing, I didn't mind someone standing on their head, it was not against the rules. However it did occur to me that he would have given me some kind of indication as to what he was going to do, as it was such an unusual thing. After about half an hour of total silence, he got back on his feet then used the chamber pot, before retiring to his bed for the night. This apparently was something he did every night before going to bed; I remember thinking to myself what a funny routine, what the hell does he get out of it, to this day I often laugh about that.

I was once in a cell in Durham and one of the lads in our cell had just been released leaving my other cell mate whose name was 'Hand'. On coming back from the workshops to our cell I noticed immediately that someone else had been moved into our cell. Believe it or not his name was 'Legg'. This was a perfect situation that appealed to my sense of humour. Legg was just starting a nine year stretch, he was eager to try to escape. I told him that if the three of us all escaped at the same time it would make one hell of a headline in the newspaper 'Escape from Durham – Mario follows Hand and Legg over the Prison Wall' or 'Hand has been taken back into custody, but Legg is still on the run', we were in stitches with laughter. We had that many laughs about that it kept us going for ages and Legg decided not to do a runner after all and serve the rest of his sentence.

Not everything in prison though was amusing. If you were on the bottom bunk, when the inmate above began to play with himself, it could be distracting. Nothing wrong with it, human nature, but distracting for others. If nature did not give humans some kind of relief, stiff sentences would be the norm and people would have to protect their butts especially from the lifers, who had not had a woman for many years. So there I was on the bottom bunk when the bloke up on top decided to sort himself out. He started off in what I would describe as first gear, which I didn't mind, in fact it was quite pleasant being rocked off to sleep having not been rocked as a child by a mother. The inmate then changed into second gear, which I could still tolerate, but when he got into third gear and then into fourth gear I was by this time getting annoyed; in fact I remember thinking "fucking hell I hope this bloke has not got ten gears". When he got into fifth gear, the bunk started banging on the cell wall, at that I lost my temper and shouted at him to sort himself out quickly, or the bloody bed was going to crash through the cell wall. It was dark, but he had tried to wait until he thought I was asleep, I told him that his timing was 'excuse the pun' all to cock and that he should start sooner and finish sooner. I mention this to stress the point that prison is not normal, it's unreal, it is pointless, it is futile and a lot of the inmates come out ten times worse than when they went in.

During my short time in prison I witnessed several suicides and one in particular was a man who cut his wrists wide open. There was blood everywhere, everyone at the time was shit scared of getting Aids and the screws told us to clean out the cell. We promptly told them to fuck off. I was once in this cell when I heard this bloke groaning. On turning round I noticed blood spreading along the white sheet he had over him. On pulling the sheet back I found him in the process of cutting his wrists, which at the end of the day was his business, but the trouble was he was using my razor blade so I proceeded to give him a bollocking. As I have said

Aids was thought to be caught easily in prison. I pressed the cell alarm or bell button and the screws came and carted him off to the hospital.

One time Harry, Micky Hay and I were entering the reception area in Durham Prison when this screw started talking down to us. At this I lost my temper and went for the screw shouting that I would kill the bastard. I chased him through the reception area, but I forgot that Micky was handcuffed to me, in the end I told the screws that we would not calm down until they got this cheeky screw away from the reception, which they readily did. I mention this because violence could and would flare up at any time and often for the slightest thing, even something that one would accept or ignore on the outside. During the short time that I have spent inside I have witnessed many incidents from stabbings, slashings to boiling water being thrown over people. I have heard it's not as bad now as a lot of inmates obtain their own calming medication either via the system or by using their own system of supply. I have heard the cries in the night of inmates who cannot bear being locked up, some sit just looking at photos of their wives and kids and I used to tell them not to dwell on their photos, but to put them away and try to keep busy. I personally filled in time learning to play the guitar and the blues harp and I even wrote songs as well "you never know they might let me out to some concert and I could do a runner'.

Rape, although not common, did occur from time to time and I have even known some young men sell their bodies for a half tin of tobacco. What would their parents have thought of that sad and depraved kind of behaviour? The sad thing though is that the system knew it was going on, but elected to turn a blind eye to this behaviour as long as the prison was quiet. I know some inmates who turned gay whilst in prison. It is completely abnormal to cage hundreds of men (some for many years) in such a small confined area as a prison. I remember one situation were I was sent to prison for something I definitely had not done, it was quite simply what can only be called a 'bum' wrap. You had to be on your toes all the time, if you dropped your new bar of soap in the showers, it was a brave man who bent down to pick it up.

When a person gets into that state of mind, it is no surprise that they have thoughts of suicide, for some strange reason it seems at the top of their minds, in cases like this it is very difficult to instil any kind of hope. One inmate did talk about death and committing suicide as he felt taking his own life would somehow make everything better and to be honest I couldn't blame him for that. Knowing what had happened with his family and how this might be effecting him I had to try to help him get himself sorted out, considering he had many years to serve he needed to get some help in getting over this. I made a comment, one that I still feel guilty about to this day. What I said to him was that in some situations or circumstances, yes death could be a release from the pain of life, especially if you had a very long stretch to do and couldn't sort out the problem that was causing the pain.

Release did come for him as three days later he committed suicide. They came for him and I will never forget the feelings I had when they placed his body in a body bag and walked passed us out of the wing. He had indeed been released from the torment and pain that had been haunting him. I have seen many body bags during my time in prison and I have also heard the cries in the night of prisoners, some who were deemed to be tough people but still cried.

It was in the late 1960s whilst I was serving a little time at Her Majesty's pleasure in Durham Prison that I came across a convicted murderer who had the physical appearance and the demeanour that suggested he wouldn't harm a fly. His name was Michael Luvaglio and he was placed in the cell next to mine. Michael had just been convicted, along with his co-accused Dennis Stafford, of the murder of gaming machine collector Angus Sibbet who was found dead with three bullets in his body on the rear seat of a Mark 10 Jaguar underneath the Pesspool Bridge in South Hetton, a mining village in County Durham, in the early hours of 5 January 1967. It was said to be the first gangland-style killing in the North East of England, prompting an MP to claim "the Mafia has arrived in the North East".

Michael Luvaglio didn't give me the impression he was a hardened villain. Michael, his co-convicted Dennis Stafford, Michael's brother Vince Luvaglio – who changed his name to Landa – and the murder victim Angus Sibbet, were all well-known faces in the North East, particularly Newcastle, Sunderland and in Weardale, but they really weren't looked upon as underworld villains, more like businessmen. They were all involved in a gambling empire based around fruit machines or one-armed bandits that Vince and his team would have installed in pubs and workingmen's clubs across the North East region, from the border with Scotland down to Teesside. It was a lucrative, cash-rich, business. It was rumoured that their little firm made as much as £3 million in their first few years of operation. The firm would also refurbish clubs and provide the entertainment, "the turns", which would attract the punters. There was much club talent in the North East at the time, such as comedians Bobby Thompson and Bobby Knoxall, who worked for Vince Landa, and singers like Ricky Hill, who had a hit record, Tony Minchella and even Dennis Stafford's girl-friend at the time, Salena Jones, a black cabaret and nightclub singer.

At the time the North East and the big towns and cities in particular had a vibrant nightlife and the workingmen from the collieries would look forward to a weekend of entertainment, and a small flutter on the one-armed bandits, after collecting their hard-earned weekly wage working at the coal face underground. For most the weekend nights in the local club were the highlights of the week. There was a big club in Byker, Newcastle, called Billy Botto's, which I would regularly attend, and this was a club frequented by many of the Newcastle faces. There were other big clubs as well, like the Dolce Vita in Newcastle.

It was at the Dolce Vita that the murder victim Angus Sibbet was last seen on the night of 4 January 1967. Someone had left him a note to meet someone at Shiney Row, not far from Sunderland, to go to a club and take the back off a bandit. This was something Angus Sibbet and others from his firm did regu-larly, collecting all the sixpences (tanners) from the machines and splitting the takings with the club steward. Of course the business was rife for theft and it was rumoured that Angus, a stocky, bearded man with a wife and mistresses, was dipping into the takings, creaming off several hundreds of pounds a week to put in his own pocket. He was certainly living the life of a high-roller, always seen in the best nightclubs and restaurants at a reserved table, buying the best champagne and eating the best meals on the menu surrounded by his lackeys and some of the women in his life. He also liked to be photographed with stars of the day, such as Tom Jones and the Winter brothers, Mike and Bernie, reflect-ing in their celebrity status glory.

When Michael Luvaglio and Dennis Stafford were jailed for his murder it seemed every face in the North East claimed to know the real background to the story. There was suggestions that someone else pulled the trigger because blood found in Angus's Mark 10 Jaguar and a phone box in South Hetton belonged neither to the victim nor the convicted men. One thing for sure is that the men were convicted on what was nothing more than circumstantial evidence based on the fact that there had been a collision between a red E Type Jaguar Dennis and Michael were using that night and the green Mark 10 Jaguar of Angus Sibbet. The defendants said they had an alibi, as they were in Newcastle's Bird Cage nightclub at the time of the murder, but the prosecution said they carried out the murder and had sufficient time to get to the Bird Cage club to establish their alibi. The police had driven from the South Hetton murder scene to the Newcastle club and, lo and behold, said it could have been done in the time-frame, despite distance involved, about ten miles, and the fact that there was a

Mario's pals, Rob Blackburn, centre, and other friends

heavy fall of snow that night. The police driver must have really been putting his foot down.

For more than 40 years the convicted killers have protested their innocence and, perhaps, it was a miscarriage of justice. I have my own theories on what happened and certainly know of other serious cases, including those of some people that I knew, whose convictions can be said to have been as watertight as a colander. On the facts, I can only give my opinion on Michael Luvaglio after his conviction, as he was in the next cell to me, and he never struck me as a killer or even a man of lesser violence. He never even lost his temper, despite his obvious frustrations and inevitable anger at being jailed for a crime he protested he never carried out. Perhaps we'll never know the real truth behind the murder because so many people around at the time are now dead, evidence will have been destroyed or corroded and memories fade.

I spent the rest of my short time in Durham Jail just waiting for the days to pass. I did a lot of reading, mostly of law books, and people in the jail began coming to me for legal advice. I developed such a good knowledge of the law some started referring to me as "Barrister John". I helped quite a number of inmates in their appeals against convictions and sentences, but more of that later.

As this book goes into print Michael Luvaglio is in his 70s and suffering from ill health and Dennis Stafford is in his 70s. Both still protest their innocence and are awaiting news of a yet another appeal. Vince Landa, now well into his 70s, is living in the south of England and is also suffering from ill health. I get the feeling that their secrets, if they have any secrets about the background to the North East's first gangland-style murder, will be taken to the grave with them. Like them, I have my own secrets that I would never divulge to anyone, or even reveal in this book. Knowledge is power and information is usually free-flowing, but some knowledge and information is so dangerous to have imparting it could really mean the difference between life and death. For now, I'd rather live until my time is due.

Despite my mistakes in life I have always been interested in what makes people tick, make no mistake about it: prison is an ideal place to make observations on people who are basically under extreme pressure twenty four hours a day, seven days a week. Especially under pressure are those inmates who have nobody or no one who will visit them, when a person first gets a very long sentence, they tend to have family or friends giving them some kind of support, however even then after a short while and in many cases the visits stop. It is people in that position who tragically end up in a body bag.

In prison I have read the original case papers of many lifers and I know for a fact that some of them should never have been convicted of murder, manslaughter maybe, but not murder. I have had a lot of experience in seeing for myself the many Queens Counsel's and Barristers who are absolutely hopeless, which is why I have personally sacked some of them. I sacked one Q.C. called Cohen, who eventually became a Judge. It is little wonder why many people are shocked at the behaviour and sentences handed out by some Judges. I have witnessed cases were it has stood out a mile that the defendant is not guilty and yet the Judges have allowed such cases to go to a jury. When the Judge has the power to stop cases of that kind it is little wonder that a lot of innocent people are suffering in prison throughout the country. What makes it all worse is that once it does become clear that a person has wrongly been convicted, it takes the judicial system years to correct the injustice, this is only because the system is reluctant to admit that perjured evidence can be given and the system is corrupt. I firmly believe that a lot of these so called learned legal people, yes they may be well educated people, do not have virtually any common sense. A lot of them are 'silver spoon' people who have come from university etc, but in reality they are total idiots who are over educated, with no experience of normal every day life, in effect they do not have a clue.

CHAPTER FIFTEEN
A PROFESSIONAL VILLAIN

At the peak of my career the world was at my feet, I was literally addicted to the buzz and the biggest buzz of them all was that every time I pulled a big job off I knew that I was giving the law and the establishment a good kick up the butt. It was that feeling that kept me going. I was really chasing the big beast or dragon, although I knew then that I could not kill it, but I certainly wounded it many times over the years. Just about every big job in the North East at that time was down to me and my merry men. We would watch the news coverage of our work on the television and read the newspaper articles that would appear in the papers. Most other villains would be guessing who was responsible and I always came into their list. I remember returning home after successfully blagging all the wages from a firm that employed many people. After splitting the dum (money) I got myself changed (clothing etc.) and was heading for home, the job had already hit the news and it was mentioned on my car radio.

I remember that I was driving along the spine road in Blaydon, near Newcastle, when I noticed a fellow villain 'Benny' coming in the opposite direction. He had also heard the news, and he gave me what I would describe as 'the look', it was a smile and a look of recognition. Of course I did not betray myself by returning the look. Although Benny was a very staunch and sound man, there are some things that a villain keeps to himself. Even the bizzies would figure it out that I was in some way responsible for that robbery, but they knew that there was nothing they could do about it because at the end of the day it is all about evidence, if they didn't have it they were fucked.

This is why they would often target me, even my then solicitor told me not to talk about my 'work' on the phone. I told him that I was well aware of that. My solicitor though was later sentenced to six years in prison and I have often meant to ask him if he had talked too much on the phone. It is ironic that he achieved something that I never did and that was being a resident in a long term prison. Many people blame their crap solicitor when they fall and get sentenced and I often wonder who he blamed. The best description of a solicitor is a 'mouth piece': that is what they are to me. I would give all the solicitors and the barristers' instructions as to exactly what they could say and make them stick to it. A lot of defendants leave their fate totally in the hands of their counsel, which is why many cases get fucked up and the poor defendants end up very unhappy with the end result of their case.

One of the first people I gleaned a lot of knowledge from was Frankie Kelly, who is in his 60s now. I used to live next door to his mam and Frankie helped get me streetwise. What a lot of people might not realise is that Frankie could look after himself. He is the fastest person I have seen at head-butting, but he never looked for trouble. Frankie Kelly was one of the cleverest men I have ever met. One North East family who were hounded by the law for years was the Sayers family. They are no longer involved in crime, but they still get hounded and yet so called pillars of society, bankers, MPs, and the like, steal millions from ordinary people and get away with it.

Over the years I have been threatened with guns, knives and iron bars. As witnesses will tell you I just attacked them on the spot, without even pausing to think. The smart ones with the guns all turned out not to be as smart as they thought, indeed after one attack I later found out that one gun wasn't even loaded. Mind you some where loaded, but the idiots that had them either didn't know how to fire, or just didn't have the bottle, to use them. The gun as I saw it was just to frighten, but it didn't frighten me not one bit. As they say the best form of attack is surprise, that's what kept me safe. I just jumped them on the spot and of course they were the ones who suffered in the end. I have always said, and held to my conviction, that if you do a job and need a gun to do it, you will suffer the consequences when you are caught. Yes, I have used guns, but only when really needed. Waving a gun at somebody is over the top; ok give them a good hiding, which although it is still violence doesn't mean that you are going to take their life away from them. Better still my belief is to do the job in and out fast, with nobody there, nobody getting hurt and more importantly nobody getting caught, that all takes careful planning and that's the name of the game – planning a smooth, fast, execution.

The first one is always the hardest, but believe me none of them were easy. Careful planning was the rule and when it comes to this, there are followers and there are leaders. Being in the latter category was my strength and the followers would have to comply with my strict standards and code of ethics. I thought to myself why do individual post ofices when we could strike at the heart of the distribution chain, this being the place were the money was sorted out ready to be transferred to the individual post offices. I thought this was a better idea and I decided to do my homework. With this in mind, what I needed to know was where the money for the post offices was coming from and it didn't take me long to find this out. I then targeted this depot to find out more. From my observations of the area around the depot where the van had returned after making it's deliveries that day, it was obvious that I needed to do more research on this place. With this paramount and forefront in my mind I found a suitable vantage point from where I could observe the routine that was unfolding in front of me. The depot itself was surrounded by a seven foot high steel security fence, this was topped with sharp spikes and to make it harder had barbed wire intertwined along its top, this was obviously there to thwart any attempts of climbing over it. However the opposite effect was that once inside the depot they also felt safe and secure. From my vantage point, which was basically a hole I had drilled through a wall, I could observe everything. The immediate impression that came into my mind was that they obviously believed that the van they were using was a secure one. Further they seemed to me to be completely at ease when they were loading it, not even suspecting for a moment that they were being watched. The entrance gates into the depot were locked, but were constantly being opened and closed as other vehicles came and went. Observing this I ignored these and concentrated on what I now referred to as the cash van. Over a period of several weeks I made a point of memorising every detail of the daily routine and followed the cash van as it made deliveries to various post offices, paying specific attention to the way the two guards worked and interacted with each other.

Watching them delivering cash bags to the post offices was by now my routine. Following them as they made their rounds and on completion returning back to the depot became my task, it was imperative that I knew every detail no matter how small. As experience in my profession has taught me there was always a weak link, it was by now my sole responsibility to find that weak link and find it I did. I observed that the two guards would start loading the cash van, obviously feeling safe and secure in the depot they didn't even glance round even when the gates were opened or closed, they just got on with the job of loading the cash. I observed that once they had loaded the cash van the driver would immediately get into the driver's side of the van, obviously waiting to go, however the other guard or colleague would then go back into the building or distribution office and would not re-appear for nearly two minutes. On returning he would immediately go straight back to the cash van and *then* lock the back door firmly; I stress the word 'THEN', because that was the weak link in their routine.

The two minutes that he always routinely took to return back into the building was the weak link as it left the cash van and all the money in it vulnerable. People may think that not locking the cash van before he went back into the building was a silly and unwise thing to do, but it has to be remembered that the guard and van were in what they obviously thought was a secure depot. Being secure in this depot they obviously did not realise that every move they made was being observed by yours truly. As you can imagine, everything was in place and in the space of that very critical two minutes we were in and out like a flash, the prize or money was fantastic and the feeling of fondling that much cash is indescribable, it was fast and efficiently carried out, with nobody getting hurt, and all that was down to careful planning and execution.

It was indeed a great deal of money, but to me it was not just all about the money, to me it was a kick in the butt for the establishment, who had treated me like an animal. It was pay back time. With every big job I carried out my mind set was, here goes 'Maggie' and Lord Norman Tebbit I am surely getting on my bike and going to work and trying my best to have a bit of the life style that you greedy ruthless bastards have. I would then think of the people who were thrust and thrown into poverty, the miners and the young people who are used by ruthless businessmen, who throw them out onto the streets when they have outlived their usefulness. It's little wonder that the youngsters today have little or no respect for the likes of them. That's the way things are and that is why I will never ever feel even a twinge of regret or guilt in what I have done in the past. In fact quite the opposite I have realised for a very long time that we are living in an 'I'm all right Jack' society and I know that I was right in what I was doing and even now I would do it all over again.

Remember it was not all about money to me, in fact I gave a lot of money away to people who were stuck in the poverty trap. I shared my spoils with less fortunate people, because I knew that not everyone could do what had in effect become second nature to me. To be a good professional in the so called crime game a person has got to have the right characteristics and mind set in their make up. Real proper villains are definitely in the minority and that minority of villains are almost born and destined to be the way they are. They are great survivors who can see through the hypocrisy of those within the establishment, and have the were-withall to choose their own destinies. They are indeed free spirits, who will not allow any system to dictate and or control their lives. Above all they are courageous people who rightly earn and get respect. In essence the true and real professionals are motivated by the injustice they witness and the corruption that they see within the system, yet they are expected to respect this. Despite the risk of years living in a cell or box, they do not want to be part of the establishment and who can blame them? Just doing the job was not always what it was all about, sometimes it was all about where the money went and the satisfaction in beating the system, it was to me in many ways all about payback.

Police surveillance photographs.

Not getting nailed is the name of the game, but I remember one incident when we were removing a safe from a post office. One of our new recruits, who was in effect an apprentice, made a terrible mistake when we were removing the safe. He managed to trap his finger in between the safe and the door and it quite unceremoniously removed the top inch of his finger! Screaming in absolute pain he was just about to take off his glove when I shouted to him do not take your glove off.

If you do they will find the top of your finger and they will have your fingerprint. At this I said they will then use it to nail us. When I remember this, thinking of his nail at the end of his severed finger I laugh, yes "They would have used that nail to nail us and it would have pointed in your direction", but it was not a joke at the time the poor sod was in absolute agony.

Sometimes there are those that just wait in the wings, waiting to pounce, waiting to catch or trap you. They are always around waiting for the opportunity to ruin everything that you have planned and worked hard for. Make no mistake, in my line of work it was hard graft, although the rewards were there for the taking. If you succeeded then it was all worthwhile, the adrenalin rush that you would get when you knew that the job was done and the rewards were there to be spent was overwhelming. Whilst I never underestimated the police, as to do that would be extremely foolish and you would definitely end up with a stretch in Durham, you couldn't always count on those around you. One of our vans was parked up at the back of one of the workingmen's clubs; it was being transferred from one place to another as we had received a tip off that the police were going to raid the yard that we had parked it in.

So here it was parked up and covered in snow, but a sharp eyed cop found it and wiping off the snow peered inside and discovered all the equipment we used on our jobs. He then reported it to the station and that was the catalyst for an investigation by the police; they had of course their informants waiting for a sniff of something that they could capitalise on, anything that they could use. But here was a van which, on checking, contained all the gear that was necessary to carry out a major job. When the young copper reported it and on checking the van out they then started an undercover operation to find out what exactly was going on. It was a chance in a million that the young copper realised what he had found and even more so when they decided to run checks on the van. They soon worked it out that they should leave it alone, putting it under surveillance.

As a result of this lucky break the police started to build up a case against us, of course they had to have either been informed, or as we later found out it was by pure chance that this cop stumbled upon the van. They followed the van to the new yard that we were going to use, it was pure chance and bad luck for us; if we had not moved the van and parked it there then they would still have been unaware of our activities. As a result of this surveillance exercise the police started to build up a case against us. Using stealth they gathered photographs of our every movement and in order to make you more aware of what they where doing we include the next section which is a transcript of the statement made by a Detective Inspector in the case that the Police were building against us, this is as follows:

[Please note names of the Officers involved change to protect their identity]

STATEMENT OF: Keith Richard Albright

AGE:	Over 21
OCCUPATION:	Detective Inspector
ADDRESS:	No. 2 Regional Crime Squad,
	Police Station, Hawthorn
	Road, Gosforth, Newcastle upon Tyne.

I am Detective Inspector No. 7309 of Northumberland Police presently seconded to the No. 2 Regional Crime Squad based at Gosforth, Newcastle upon Tyne.

On the following dates the below listed Post Offices were subject of burglaries:-

Date	Post Office
22.02.89	Plumstead Rd Post Office, Norwich.
07.03.89	Bog Hall Post Office, West Lothian, Scotland.
27.09.89	Ladyton Post Office, Falkirk, Scotland.
28.11.89	Ladysmill Post Office, Falkirk, Scotland.
10.04.90	Gorgie Road Post Office, Edinburgh, Scotland.

The method by which the Post Offices were subject to burglary had a common characteristic amongst them all, in that, alarms fitted with foam to render them inaudible, telephone wires were cut to the attacked premises, the doors were forced and a safe removed as opposed to other burglaries at Post Offices were entry was different; and the safe had been attacked and left on the premises.

Certain links with Tyneside and the offences were discovered, more prominently the recovery of the safe from Plumstead Road, Norwich, at Whitehouse Road, Newcastle upon Tyne and the safe from Bog Hall Post Office recovered in Gatehead, Tyneside. Large quantities of the negotiable property stolen from all the offences turned up on Tyneside i.e. Postal Orders, Stamps, Television Stamps etc. The total value stolen during these burglaries was £547,386. Following the connection with the burglaries and Tyneside, No. 2 Regional Crime Squad based at Gosforth, Newcastle upon Tyne, commenced enquiries into the offences.

On Wednesday 13th February, 1991 an operation was mounted, centered upon a Ford Transit van, displaying Reg. No. F868 PHD, situated in A.A. Builders Suppliers Yard, Old Railway Goods Yard, Quayside, Newcastle upon Tyne. This operation consisted of a twenty four hour continuous surveillance on the van. I was continually informed each day about the surveillance. At 1.30 p.m. on Tuesday 5th March 1991 as a result of what I heard and was told I was collected by Detective Constable 202 WILSON and with Detective Constable WILSON we drove south on the A1(M) where we caught up and took part in a surveillance on the van, bearing registration number G748 RJR, a white Nissan Sunny car bearing registration number G150 WTY and a beige Ford Escort, bearing registration number D765 YLR, which were travelling together in convoy. The surveillance continued to New Lakenham Post Office situated at Queen's Road, Norwich.

The police surveillance operation, I have to say, seemed quite professional. I ended up at court for conspiracy to burgle. Myself and three others were stopped on our way to Scotland were I am very confident that had we not been stopped we would have secured two million cigarettes. For each million we would have received £48,000. I know that because during the course of my professional career I had successfully secured millions of cigarettes which had always paid well.

We were travelling with two stolen vans and a stolen car. With us we had all the necessary, for example a scanner and radios. We wanted to make sure that we knew what the police were up to. Well we got stopped and seeing this lot the game was up, we eventually ended up back again at the Crown Court, of course as usual the Police had me down as the main player due to my past history. A sentence of around five to six years would have been the normal time for this under the circumstances. My barrister came down to the cells below the Court wanting to discuss any mitigation he might be able to say about me before any sentencing. He thought it would be a straight guilty plea, that it was a cut and dry case, but to his absolute amazement I told him that my plea would be not guilty. I told him that it was my legal right to put my case over in front of a jury and that they would decide my fate. He reminded me that if I pleaded not guilty it could and would probably get me an even longer prison sentence. He said that the Judge would feel that I was wasting court time, not to mention the cost of a long trial. My co-accused were on bail at the time, they did not turn up at the Court and warrants were put out for their arrests. This of course all added to the confusion, so I stuck to my "guns" not guilty was my plea, looking rather perplexed he said that he would notify the Court that I was pleading not guilty. He obviously didn't know that I knew that he was actually going to see the Judge in the Judges chambers. When he came back down to see me my barrister said that he felt very confident that my sentence would be less than six years, without telling me what made him so confident. My plan was beginning to work and I again told my barrister that I was going to plead not guilty; he again disappeared up the stairs without saying anything. A short while later he again returned and said well what about four years how does that sound, my reply was that I still intended to plead not guilty. He was looking even more puzzled and by this time he was getting more flustered and beads of sweat were running down his fore-head, so much so that he went to wipe his head causing his wig to fall off onto the floor. He hurriedly put it back on to his head and it wasn't on right. When I think that he had to pass an area where people were standing around including witnesses it still makes me laugh. One of the people he had to pass was my wife Glady and she was by now getting a bit confused as well on seeing my barris-ter. She noticed that he was looking and getting more flustered the more he passed her. She remembers him passing her still in the process of trying to get his wig on straight. Glad asked him what was happening, he replied 'when I go back down to see Mario I hope he takes my advice'. Glad told me later that she couldn't stop laughing as his wig was still lying askew on his head, which by this time we knew was bald. Someone should have given him a mirror to save his embarrassment. On coming back down to the cells to see me again he had completely lost the plot and his barrister image, in fact he looked a downright shambles and appeared to be sweating a lot, then he seemed to struggle getting his words out. By this time I knew I had him where I wanted him. He then blurted out obviously dreading what my answer was going to be he said "What about three years?" so I finally put him out of his misery and shouted loud and clear "Guilty as Charged". The look of relief on his by now red and sweating face was a sight to behold, at this he inadvertently farted at least twice, as he literally ran along the passage from the cells, as he did this his black cloak was hovering up off the floor behind him, I could not resist shout-ing after him "I will see you up in Court Batman!".

I got three years and I was aware that the Judge had no choice but to keep to his word. Remember there was another three men coming his way, who may also plead not guilty. He also had to think of the barristers, and high blood pressure can be dangerous. As an explanation and moral to the above many of the people who know me will tell of how often I have said, if you know that you cannot win a court case the next best thing is to confuse and complicate the issue in such a way that you keep the length of the sentence down to as low as possible. It is essential though that to do that you have got to know how the system works, only then can a person gain the advantage against what I prefer to call the enemy. It is no coincidence that despite being a very active villain for three decades I have not seen the inside of a long term prison.

I know that is not always easy to get to know the various establishments and systems, because believe it or not England is one of the most secret countries in the world.

The example that I have given you above of what goes on behind the scenes in the courts is all to do with mind games. In America I would not have had to confuse or complicate the issue because the legal system there is a lot more honest and open. It is openly and publicly called *plea bargaining* whereas in our legal system it is done in an underhand and sly way. Only those who study how the system works and who have the imagination and the wherewithal to take advantage of the dishonest and secretive ways of the legal system will beat them at their own game. It reminds me of an old saying "It takes a rogue to catch a rogue", and believe me there are many rogues within the legal system and other organizations. I know this because I have met a lot of these hypocrites, at least a villain has the courage to be on the front line, and they don't have to, nor need to, hide behind a large establishment to commit crime. That is just one of the reasons a lot of people have a kind of respect for the proper villains. Remember there are villains with principles and there are villains with absolutely no principles, and there is a vast difference between the two.

In another police operation in which I was targeted two of my pals and I were stopped on a dual carriageway by the police. In our car they found what they deemed to be tools that could be used for crime, and we got charged with going equipped for burglary. It was a stupid and flimsy charge, but the police could do it because we had criminal records. If there was even a screw driver in a car the police would automatically charge people with form. The nearest Magistrates Court was in a very small town. There we went before the Magistrates and they had no hesitation in remanding us in custody to Durham Prison. This was in the 1970's and that time it was compulsory for the Prison to produce all remanded prisoners before the Magistrates Court.

It was in the middle of summer and very warm. Due to my illness, which makes it extremely difficult to stand the heat, after two or three weeks of going back and forth to the Magistrates and knowing all the time that the Magistrates had no intention of granting us bail at all, I was by now fed up and sick of being crammed into a small van. I knew that I would much rather be left at Durham jail until the case came to be heard. I put it to the other lads that the next week we were going to go to the Court I was not going to move from my cell and I was going to refuse to go up to the Court. I discussed this with the other lads, they were giving it a bit thought when one of them (Dave) said, his wife was upstairs in the Court hoping that we would get bail. Dave said what about my wife? I remember saying to him fuck your lass, you know these Magistrates are just messing us about and that they were taking no notice of our solicitors. I told him to have a bit of courage and that if we stick together we would be letting the Magistrates know that we have no interest in them or their Court. Dave asked what would happen when the warders came down to the cell and ordered us to go up to the Court. I told him that I did not know, but whatever happens we must stand our ground. I did not know what would happen as I had never known people to defy Court Orders in this way. I myself was not too worried about getting bail, all I wanted was for them to stop trailing me back and forth from jail to the Court every seven days, only to face Magistrates who just sent us back. It was an absolute farce and above all it was not doing my illness any good at all. To give both the lads credit the lads decided to go ahead with my decision and refused to go up to the Court. I instructed my solicitor to tell the Court that I just wanted to be left at Durham jail and further if there was any change of circumstance to just send the message to Durham jail. I said just send it to landing three, cell number 2T.

One of the lads Micky H, knew that I was not happy being stuck in vans to face a court who just sent us back. I am sure it was just the week before that I snapped and rushed towards a prison screw and would have killed the bastard if he had not ran away. Unfortunately, I had forgotten that Mick H was handcuffed to me, but Mick would tell anyone that the screw I went to attack acted like a little Hitler. Other screws were asking us to calm down. We told them we would not calm down until they got rid of that bastard screw, from the reception area, which of course they did. I have got to say that Mick H, unlike me, was a very street wise guy, this due to me being cocooned all of my childhood in the home, hostel and borstal. I was not familiar with many things about the villainy game, Mick and I started off a bit small time, but we always got by, as time went on we made a fortune. In fact in today's money it would run into a couple of million, we seemed to gel together. I was handy with safes and alarms and Micky could enter a place with ease and bottle, with Micky being small and light he could almost slip under a door and he was always as quite as a mouse. We were very successful and I have some great memories of the years that we worked together, we both went on to become the biggest money earners in the North East of England.

I could write a book on its own about the time that Mick H and I worked together, but one case stands out above all the rest. We had received information that there was a safe full of cash in this very rich man's big posh house, what we did not realise was that we had been infiltrated by a police informer. The informer who had worked with us before seemed a sound guy, which is why we did not suspect anything, when at the last minute he told us that he was unable to attend the job mentioned above. The target house was on it's own in the countryside, and for that reason we told our driver to drive past the house every few minutes in the event of getting a scatter. What we did not know was that the police were hiding in a small upstairs bedroom. When you are doing a job of that kind, it is important to make sure that you are able to get out of the place. On entering the house Harry 'M' and I went to unlock and open a couple of windows at the same time Micky 'H' started to make his way up a long staircase, then just as Harry and I got to the bottom of the staircase we heard a noise and shouting. On glancing up the top of the stairs, we could see that Micky was being pinned down by several men, this happened within a split second and instinct told us that we had been set up.

The important reason why I am mentioning this incident is that no villains seemed to have a worked out plan on what to do under these kind of circumstances. It seemed to be the accepted rule that if it 'comes on top' as we say in the game, it was simply a case of get out quick. Everyone had to look after himself and try to get away, like the time Harry, Micky and I were doing a job, and I was on a small roof dismantling an alarm system. Both Harry and Mick were just below me watching me doing the alarm, when all of a sudden a police panda car appeared from round the corner and spotted us. Harry and Mick immediately ran off and I was caught and ended up getting twelve months in Leeds Prison. I did not give the police my name because if I had done the Leeds police would have contacted the police in Newcastle and I knew that if they did they would know that we were working together. Harry and Mick would probably have been nicked before they got home. I have always felt uneasy in situations like what I have mentioned above. The question is do you attack the police violently with crow bars or the like risking many years in jail, or is it better if one gets nicked and gets a quick twelve months sentence? I suppose the latter is the common sense thing to do, it's a tricky one which I have already said has always made me feel uneasy.

Getting back to the house where we were caught. Harry and I quickly turned around and ran out of the side door from which we had entered. We ran along the driveway of the house, I ran straight for a field and I got behind a hedge which concealed me from were the house was. It was daylight so I had to keep my head down as I ran further from the house. When I got far enough away I lay low until it got dark, then got myself to a phone box where I asked my brother-in-law to pick me up. I was about twenty miles away from Newcastle and with all of this happening so quickly I did not know which way Harry went, but I later learned that when he had ran to the end of the driveway he turned right. At that point according to Harry he felt a blow to the back of his head. He said that one of the police had thrown a truncheon from some distance away which had hit him smack in the back of his head knocking him down and almost knocking him out, which in turn caused him to get nicked. I wondered what had happened to the driver who as it turned out had passed the target house a couple of times whilst we were making our entry. It turned out that as he neared the house he saw Mick and Harry being held by several police, as a result all he could do was drive on and make his way from the area and return to Newcastle.

It seemed obvious to me that the police would know that I was no doubt there with Harry and Mick, but the question was what evidence they would have. Once I learned later that there were no cameras and no forensics I knew that all they could say was that they had seen me. I was of course on the run, I was laying low. I needed to find out what I could from Harry and Mick who by this time had been given a week on remand. The following week though both Harry and Mick got bail and sure enough one of the police was going to say that they had seen me. This cop was an inspector. Harry, Mick and myself were discussing who the informer was. We knew it was not the driver as he had been asked to come on the job until the very last minute, in fact he did not even known where the job was until we got there. We could not adjourn the job because we were told that the house was very rarely dead (no one at home), which is why it had to be done that day. We knew that the informant was either the card marker, the man who gave the information to us regarding the safe in the house, or it was our so called pal who had chosen not to come on the job at the last minute. His name was Jimmy. At the time I was staying not far away in a caravan at a place called Crimdon Dene near Hartlepool. I am not very good at remembering dates, but I do remember that it was 1976, and it was the hottest summer I can remember in my life. Word soon got out and around in the underworld grapevine that Jimmy was a suspected informer.

One day soon after, Harry was driving slowly in Newcastle City Centre when all of a sudden the passenger door opened and a gun was pointed to his head. It was Jimmy. He told Harry that it must have been the card marker who had grassed us up and that he was carrying the gun to protect himself. I knew that he had produced the gun hoping that I would be reluctant to pursue him and he knew for sure that Harry would tell me about the gun incident. The first thing I did was to have the card marker picked up by a couple of my heavyweight mates. He was taken to a prearranged place where, without going into too great a detail, it was established that he was not the informer. We then received very good and true information about Jimmy that corroborated what I had always suspected. Jimmy was never seen again, he just seemed to disappear into thin air.

I eventually got caught and was remanded for the above mentioned house job. They caught me after I was spotted in a car with my brother Frank who is a fantastic driver. Loads of police cars seemed to come out from nowhere, they chased us just about all over Hartlepool. Eventually though they cornered us and I jumped out of the car and tried to get away by running over gardens, jumping walls etc., but to no avail, there was just too many cops and to be honest I can only run fast for a short distance. I got bail after a while. I then received two committal papers (case against me) and sure enough the case rested on nothing more than whether this police inspector had seen me. With it being daylight it was obvious that the cops would have to have hidden themselves or we would have seen them. When they had jumped on Mick 'H' at the top of the stairs apparently not to be seen they had hidden themselves together in a small bedroom. It was established that the window in this room was closed, yet this Inspector said on oath that he could look down from the closed window and see me down below outside and that I was looking through a downstairs back window.

George Craig, Frankie Kelly, Mario.

Before the case started I had instructed my solicitor to find out by going to the house to see exactly if it was possible to see a person directly below the upstairs window. He sent out a private detective who reported back that it was impossible to see anything below. The inspector could not say that he had his big head sticking out of the window in broad daylight, when the intruders would easily have seen him. I had told my barrister the only sure way of proving this point was for the judge and jury to go to the house and look for themselves and that is exactly what happened. We set off from Durham Crown Court in a convoy of vehicles. Judge Myrella Cohen, the prosecution barristers, my defence team and myself and most important of all the jury, all travelled to the house. When we got to the house I remember the judge and the jury going upstairs to the back bedroom. They came out of the house after only a few minutes and when we got back to the court the judge said to the jury that having seen the window situation it is clear that the police inspector is mistaken as nothing can be seen below the window. She then went on to say to the jury that there is no evidence to convict, she then turned to me and said that I could go. I then shouted out to the judge and jury that a very serious offence of perjury had been committed by the police inspector. I said that he should be charged and imprisoned, but as usual nothing happened to the inspector and yet if I, or any ordinary person, had been seen to be committing perjury or lies on oath, we would have been charged and jailed. When a friend of mine Frankie Kelly was found guilty of perjury he was sentenced to three years in jail.

The moral of the above case is that when the police commit deliberate perjury it is called a mistake, but when an ordinary member of the public is deemed to have committed perjury they get years in jail. The reason why I have explained the above case is to reinforce why I have no respect for the courts, judges and the police and I feel a great sympathy for all of those who get wrongly convicted and are suffering in prison and their families as well. When the system corruptly stitches some innocent person up they have the audacity to call these many cases a miscarriage of justice, but they are often premeditated, corrupt and serious injustices, carried out in order to get a conviction. To me that is evil behaviour and the people responsible for ruining so many lives, those of innocent people, should be jailed for many years as a result of their lies and perjury.

It is rather like making me the judge on other villains. We know that these systems are evil and wicked, but we are essentially powerless to do anything about it. The people within these establishments are despicable cowards, who hide behind the shield of the establishment they do the dirty work for. I personally was involved in a case that was from the top to the bottom full of lies, deceit and corruption, a case that the end result of which would seriously affect vulnerable innocent people. The judge knew that it was a pack of lies that he was hearing, because is stuck out a mile, even a ten year old child would be able to reach the conclusion that it was nothing less than a corrupt case, but this judge decided to go with the current system, which has had a terrible affect on innocent people to this day. At the end of the case I told the judge that all those who were involved in this sad case, including him, should be taken out and put against a wall and shot. The judge stood up and saying nothing, with his head bowed, headed down to the judges chambers. I am supposed to be a villain, but I could never live with myself if I were guilty of injustices such as what transpired in this case. Remember injustices do occur on a regular basis. All I have said above should explain why I deeply distrust and dislike authority and also why myself and other people like me who understand how evil these people can be, have absolutely no respect for any of them. Who can blame us.

The main reason for such cock ups is that many people do not take the time to study how the legal system works, they just leave it all to one bloke. This is a big mistake as the man employed, at the end of the day, does not really give a fuck about the defendant or the defendant's family. When the defendant gets put down to begin a jail term the lawyer just buggers off home to prepare for his next case, its all down to money at the end of the day, as long as the lawyer gets the 'big' fat cheque he is happy, that's the way I see it, because that is the way it is. Once people realise that it is a "I'm all right Jack" society, they will then know that it is down to them, and them only, as to whether they stand or fall and I am very happy to say that I am still standing.

From the time I fell and cracked my head I have never once allowed the legal system to take control over my destiny, to cause me to fall in a big way and that was not achieved by good luck. I had a philosophy, a strategy, which I stuck too, dare I say rebelliously. There are many ways to fuck the system. The police and legal system also have many ways in which they are experts to fuck the villain. There is plenty of documented evidence that the police have been known to plant evidence on people, and in my day they did this regularly to people: in our terminology they 'verbled' us, that is making false representations as to what a suspect is supposed to have said during questioning. They even wrote statements of confessions, then got the suspects to sign the statements.

Amanda, Andrea, Gladys, Darren

I had already helped some people in jail win their cases with my legal knowledge or even have their sentences reduced compared to what they would have received on a guilty plea. On the outside one case involved my son Darren defending an aggravated burglary charge. While Darren, my wife Glad, and me, were in the waiting area just outside the court room within Newcastle Crown Court the prosecuting barrister came out of the court to tell Darren that there would be a short delay for the case to commence. On seeing me standing near to Darren and Glad the barrister asked them "is that Mario?" pointing in my direction. When they said yes the barristers said "we call him the case wrecker" and then he turned and kind of smiled at me as he returned back into court.

About 20 minutes later he came back into the waiting area and told Glad and Darren he would not be taking the case on after all and the case was later adjourned. He later told Glad and Darren the reason he had sacked himself was because of me.

It had been rumoured that I had won cases by influencing witnesses and nobbling juries. Correct me if I am wrong but surely that is part of a top villain's job. The police and many of their witnesses commit perjury on a regular basis which is why many innocent people ended up convicted for crimes they did not commit. At the end of the day I was only doing my duty evening up the scales of justice, which is what the courts are supposed to do.

Wherever I see injustice I will do my utmost to expose the legal system and the corrupt and underhand way it crushes and seriously ruins the lives of the ordinary public. Even the wigs and the black batman cloaks they wear and the sinister atmosphere in court are designed to intimidate ordinary people. I can see right through them, which is why they were never too keen on me advising or being involved in cases.

Two of my pals and I did a bank job which was situated about 150 miles away from Newcastle. We knew that the time lock released itself on the vault which then allows the manager to open the vault with a big key. I managed to grab an

Mario and Darren

hour-and-a-half's kip while we waited for the bank manager, which was good for my medical condition. What the manager did not know was that we were already concealed in the bank and had rendered the alarm and the CCTV cameras useless. We let him go to the alarm panel to switch the alarm off, but he didn't know it was already switched off as we had adjusted the panel so that when he turned the panel key the light turned from green to red, which is certainly how it worked in those days. After a very short time we heard the time lock releasing itself and we allowed him to open the big steel doors of the vault. It was then that we appeared and dealt with him as we had to before we filled three big holdalls full of cash. We locked the manager in a room at the back of the bank, knowing that other bank staff would be arriving at any time. When we emerged from the bank we almost bumped into two staff who had just got out of a car. Our car was in sight of the two staff and for that reason we decided not to use it. We done a few lefts and rights and found a sweet place to conceal the cash. We got ourselves a couple of miles away then I contacted one of my partners, who was a sound and tested and staunch woman, and she came and got us and the cash out of the area and back home.

I used to like working away from Newcastle because I knew I would not be in the frame. I can imagine the headlines that would have appeared in some of the local newspapers where the bizzies would have been looking for local villains.

The last few jobs I was involved in were what we called sweet work, where there was no threats or violence or actual violence. The jobs were mainly post offices and out of one of them alone we got 120 grand, which would be worth a quarter of a million now. We done a good number of them but we got nicked. The bizzies were just lucky when a young plod who noticed our van which needed to be moved from A to B. The yard we originally used was also where the safes were opened but on a couple of occasions they were not fully destroyed so when the bizzies finally nicked us for just one post office they tried to tie us in with others. The yard disposal men had gotten a bit lazy, they were normally very efficient. Two of them were penalised financially. The post office jobs were the last of my career and we made a good deal of money. After serving a quick three stretch in jail the drug scene took over the crime game and that was not a scene for me. I quietly retired, but people were still knocking on my door for a natter.

CHAPTER SIXTEEN

JOHN THE BARRISTER

I have personally trapped and proved that policemen have committed perjury in Court, but no charge was ever brought against them. The legal system bends over backwards to avoid having to charge them. In my younger days I had concealed some jewellery in a place were the police found it. I was charged with handling swollen property, sorry stolen property. Amongst the jewellery were two three carat good quality diamonds, but when I got the court papers which listed the items or 'Tom' as we called it, the two diamonds were not listed they were 'missing'. I really did not mind as it reduced the value of the 'stolen' jewellery to almost half of the amount. They say that diamonds are forever and I often wonder if that member of the police force has still got them.

People should have a non violent revolution, they should toughen up the fight for equality and justice. It is not necessary to use violence to bring the country almost to a complete stand still. Unlike us, the French are strong in mind, while we are weak. This is why the government and all the other damned establishments in this country have a free reign to do exactly what they want to do, safe in the knowledge that we, the British public, are weak and a feeble people, who will not challenge them vigorously.

In another travesty of justice, for example, in my last case the police had us bang to rights for attempted burglary of another Post Office. We were all totally prepared to plead guilty, but when we got the deposition papers (the case against us), and there inside the bundle were another two sets of papers which mentioned a further six Post Offices in which over half a million pounds had been taken. The papers on these did not have one scrap of evidence to say that we had been involved or indeed had been responsible for these. On realising this I immediately instructed my lawyers to have these legally removed and deleted from the deposition papers, as we had not been charged with them in the first place. I am fully aware that the Judge reads all the papers before a case and I also knew that I was to be sentenced for one Post Office job. The Judge would have read about the six other Post Offices and believe me that he would have reflected on the sentences taking these into account in a big way. I firmly believe that is why the police corruptly placed the details on the six other Post Office robberies in with our desposition papers for the Judge to see and thereby to increase our sentences. I was also aware that the Judge's own staff and the other court staff would have no doubt already have had an opportunity to have read these and knowing how corrupt the police are, I just knew that despite these being legally deleted from the bundle the police would find someway in slipping them back in.

Taking that into consideration, when we went to court for sentencing our barristers thought it would be a straightforward guilty plea. However on seeing our barristers I immediately asked them why the Judge had read the pages relating to the six Post Office robberies. The barrister said, how can we be sure what papers have been read by the Judge in this case and at that I told him that my instructions to him were to ask the Judge in court if he had read the disputed papers. I then added, we will see if the Judge is a liar or corrupt then; the Barrister appeared to be amazed that I knew the workings of what goes on in the Judges chambers. I told the Barrister that once the Judge admits that he had indeed read the disputed papers I wanted a full investigation into the handling of the whole case. I then told him that our case should then be heard before a fresh court and definitely in front of a different Judge.

Once in Court my barrister followed my instructions and asked the Judge if he had read the disputed papers, the ones that had been legally removed as they were not pertinent to our case. The Judge knew that he had to either tell a lie in open Court with other people there knowing about the papers we were talking about. He had no other choice other than to admit that he had indeed read the papers prior to these being legally removed and then just as quickly these illegally being slipped back into the deposition papers. The Judge was looking rather flustered and shocked by this request; he obviously did not know what to say and he adjourned the case for a few hours. You have to remember that for burgling a Post Office it was the normal practice to sentence those involved for between six and seven years and that's just for one Post Office. If the police had got away with this stroke, we would have received a very long sentence as the Judge would no doubt have taken all of them into consideration during sentencing. After a short while our barristers approached us and indicated that the Judge was prepared to be lenient and fair in our case under all the circumstances. We all ended up getting three years, which in effect meant that we would only have to serve around eighteen months. With my remand time taken off I was free within months. During the hearing though a police inspector was caught telling lies on oath, so I shouted loud and clear in front of the Judge that this inspector was a perjurer and it was little wonder that so many innocent people are in prison. I am not sure if the Judge was amused by this, or angry, but at the end of the day he didn't go over board with the sentences so we must have made an impact.

One of the top men in Chester-le-Street, a County Durham town not far from Newcastle, was Frankie Dunbar, who I became quite friendly with. Frankie ran most of the doors in the town, or employed the men who did, and one of the doormen was a young amateur boxer called Liddle Towers, who was killed by police in one of the worst cases of police brutality I have ever come across. I knew Liddle, who was a staunch and loyal man, and he didn't deserve to die. The fact that not one police officer faced criminal charges over his shocking and brutal death is sadly indicative of the world in which we live, where's there's one law for the powers that be and another law for the rest of us.

Liddle died on 9 February 1976 at Dryburn Hospital in Durham, from serious and severe injuries he received at the hands of the police only three or so weeks earlier. He had been arrested outside the Key Club at Birtley, Gateshead, near Chester-le-Street, and after a violent struggle, when most of the violence was directed at him by no fewer than eight police officers, he was put into a dog van and taken to Gateshead police station. Later, at 4 am, he was taken from the station to Queen Elizabeth Hospital because he complained of not feeling well, and, after an examination which apparently revealed no injury and nothing wrong with him, he was taken back to the cells. He was discharged later that same morning at 10 o'clock. Both the taxi driver who took Liddle home and his local GP, Dr. Powney, who saw him later that day at 2 o'clock, gave evidence at a later inquest that was consistent with Liddle's own account of having been assaulted in the cells. Liddle told a friend: "They gave us a bloody good kicking outside the Key Club, but that was nowt to what I got when I got inside." That evidence, of course, could not be heard at the inquest. It was considered 'hearsay'.

Liddle was a 39-year-old electrician and a well-known and popular man in Chester-le-Street. He was a man with a strong physical presence and a formidable strength of character. But he was never a violent man. He had no previous criminal record for acts of violence. Indeed, apart from motoring offences the only criminal record he had was for the theft of £3 worth of scrap metal.

At the inquest into his death on 8 October 1976, a verdict of 'justifiable homicide' was returned. That was a very strange verdict. Taken literally, it meant that the police intended to kill Liddle Towers and were justified in so doing. How the fuck can that be? How the fuck can it be justified that a man arrested for drunkenness (Liddle) who was set upon by a gang of eight burly fucking police officers, who acted like a pack of bloodthirsty fucking savages, were 'justified' in fucking killing him. He was one man who put up a struggle when he was arrested. One fucking man!

Later, the local MP Giles Radice, asked the then Home Secretary, Merlyn Rees, for a full inquiry into Liddle's death. Guess what Mr Rees's response was? The cause of Mr Towers' death, he said, and allegations that Northumbria police officers dealing with him committed offences of violence had been fully investigated in accordance with the proper processes of law. The Director of Public Prosecutions concluded, Mr Rees added in the House of Commons, that after careful consideration of the outcome of those investigations and after consulting leading counsel, that this was not a case in which criminal proceedings should be instituted against any police officer. This was also the conclusion reached by the Attorney-General, who also indicated that all the medical experts who had been consulted were agreed that there was no medical evidence to support a contention that Mr Towers' death was in any way attributable to wilful violence or rough handling by the police. Bit of a pattern here, don't you think? People in power protecting people in power who fucking killed a man in the prime of his life for no fucking reason other than they liked to hit people, very hard? This was the most disgraceful case of a cover-up, a fucking whitewash by the powers-that-be and it makes me so, so, angry when I think about it.

Other people were just as angry and didn't stop thinking about it. A local punk band, the Angelic Upstarts, brought out a single record "Who Killed Liddle?", which made the top 40, and they played it around the club circuit with their lead singer kicking a pig's head around on stage. The band were managed by a South Shields villain who had become a thorn in the side of the police over several years, Keith Bell.

A year into his tenure as Northumbria's Chief Constable, Sir Stanley Bailey became embroiled in the controversial case. Bailey maintained that a newspaper article in November 1977 highlighting the Towers case had wrecked his chances as a candidate for the post of Commissioner of the City of London force, but his complaint to the Press Council was rejected. Maybe he should have kept a stronger leash on his out-of-control, psychopathic police officers.

I was in Durham Jail on remand at the same time as Keith Bell, who was known as a hard man but basically didn't know his own limitations when it came to violence and his chosen opponents. Keith Bell and a friend of his in the jail, Arthur Tams, of the well-known Tams crime family in Newcastle, were the bully boys of the prison shop. They were both violent men and Arthur Tams later died a violent death when he was shot by a relative and battered to death with a baseball bat. In the jail they ruled by fear, and many inmates kept a wide berth of both of them.

A great friend of mine, with whom I had done some work with in the past, was also in Durham Jail at the time, serving his longest prison sentence of eight years for a long-firm fraud and a tie-up robbery that had gone arse over tit because of two plonkers on the team. George Craig, nicknamed Butchy, was a staunch and loyal friend and considered the 'Godfather' of Sunderland. He had set up a company called Crunchox Ltd, with references from a few business friends, including a fruiterer's in Newcastle and a florist's in Sunderland, trading in everything from paper towels to televisions and no sooner had the goods arrived in the warehouse they were out again on the black market. Buying goods on credit which you couldn't, or wouldn't, pay for was not good business, of course. A criminal bankruptcy followed and George and a few others were done for obtaining goods by deception. George was in

Durham Jail at the time awaiting the Crunchox trial to start, at the same time as an old friend of his Stuart Mottram, also known as Benny the Brick, and a friend of both of ours, Freddie Mills, known as 'Fred the Head' from Newcastle. George told me the story of how Benny got his nickname. He had been walking along Fawcett Street, the main shopping street in Sunderland, near Christmas with his girlfriend, when his lass spotted a smart coat in a shop window and asked him to get it. Benny threw a brick through the window and grabbed it. Then she saw a bike for a young lad and Benny grabbed a brick, smashed the window, and grabbed the bike. This went on until almost all their Christmas shopping was done. Finally they passed a jewellers and the lass asked for a nice ring. "Do you think I'm made of fucking bricks!" Benny asked.

I digress. At this time Keith Bell, the so-called 'Sheriff of South Shields', was letting his mouth go, claiming he was going to 'sort out' George, for no other reason than to inflate his own ego as one of the most violent men on the wing. Keith Bell was a hard man, but no match for George Craig, and disrespecting a good friend of mine like George was something I couldn't tolerate. I wasn't about to have a go at Keith Bell, because I knew George could eat the man alive and spit his bones out. I tipped George off that Keith Bell was going to have a go at him and George, always the coolest of characters under pressure, just bided his time, waiting for Keith Bell to pounce. It happened soon after in one of the recesses. Keith Bell jumped George, mouthing off loudly, and George just turned and gave him the biggest good hiding he had ever suffered. A battered, bloodied and bruised Keith Bell came to me later with his tail between his legs and said: "He pulled all my fucking hair out!" I said: "You're lucky he didn't pull your fucking head off, you daft cunt!"

George and I kept in touch during our prison stays and afterwards on the outside and he was there in my greatest hour of need when I had reached the pits of despair because of my heavy cocaine use. But more of that later.

A recent example of serious injustice was when one million people stood out in protest against the war in Iraq, no member of the Government even bothered to come out and to at least acknowledge the people, they just totally ignored them. After a while the million protestors just meekly headed for home, then the war went ahead. So much for our democracy. A genuine democracy is a system where we vote these people into representing us, to listen to us, to cause change for us, but the very people that we put in power treated those million people with total disdain and disrespect. The million people that had gathered there completely wasted their time, they just stood around like a herd of docile cattle whilst the Government took no notice of them at all. This feeble attempt to exercise their 'democratic' right proved without doubt that we kid ourselves into believing that we live in a great democratic country. I believe that is living in cloud cuckoo land, in fact some of our prime ministers have proved to be no more than dictators, because dictators do exactly what they want despite what the people want, that feels like a dictatorship to me.

I feel that it was beyond the wit of our special forces to have removed the main players in Iraq, after thrashing out a plan to ensure a better system that could have been put into place, but they wanted full control of Iraq itself, thereby having control of the massive oil fields and further getting a big foothold in the Middle East. I do not blame them for that, but what disturbed me was that they did not tell the truth of the real motives for the war. I believe that, if they had been honest, many people would have understood why it may well have been necessary to take care of an extremely dangerous and loose cannon who was the dictator in Iraq, who could very well have got control of most of the oil in the World. If that had been allowed to happen we car owners would literarily have to get on our bikes. Although I personally would just walk because with my criminal record you can be sure that I would get done for peddling or an alternative charge of pushing, even at my age they just will not leave me alone.

As this book goes into print the New Labour Government has refused to disclose what was said in Cabinet meetings by ministers about the reasons we went into war with Iraq. They have decided it would not be in the public interest to know this information. And they have refused to divulge it under the Freedom of Information Act. An Act this very same Government introduced, claiming it would make our democratic process more open and accountable. Yes, multi millions of British taxpayers money has been spent on the war; yes, hundreds of British soldiers have been killed; yes, there are still hundreds of other soldiers both British and American who will be killed, but no, we can't know the real reasons why we went to war in the first place. If that's democracy, I'm the head of the Roman Catholic Church.

CHAPTER SEVENTEEN
THE GEORDIE UNDERWORLD

Technically, at that time, the world of crime was going through massive changes, with innovation being the key, with new high tech cameras and alarm systems being brought in to fight the ever increasing amount of crime. It was nothing less than a deliberate attempt by the Government to reduce the number of robberies that were taking place on a regular basis. To a large extent the Government bragged that crime was being controlled and indeed reduced by a large percentage, when in fact the villains were getting more sophisticated and smarter in their chosen line of work. I remember predicting at the time that violent crime would increase and that it would get a lot worse, it was obvious that certain people, who were up to that time 'non violent' would succumb to becoming increasingly more violent to achieve their aims.

Personally, I knew many who felt that the only way to supplement their meagre Giro, was to turn to violent crime. So, while the Government preached and stressed what a good job it was doing in reducing crime, in the end it had to admit that violent crime had nearly doubled. More and more of the public became victims of serious violence and the murder rate soared, with more people obtaining firearms or even a simple baseball bat, which in itself could cause a lot of damage. It was in my opinion that the Government had got it all wrong and I personally would rather be a victim of 'non violent' crime instead of being shot, battered, mugged or left for dead. I believed it was both stupid and unfair that we had a system upheld by the Government of the haves and have nots. There will always be crime; we live in a greedy society. It's particularly galling when you consider that MPs actually decide for themselves how much extra they are going to increase their salaries by. We are all aware of the corruption in Government, they steal from us by fiddling their expenses, which is nothing less than theft. The problem now is that young people, due to better communication, see and know what's happening by the people we are expected to respect without question.

Liars and conmen, you don't have to look far for them, they are on your television every day and night. We unfortunately could have put them there by voting for them, but when they are caught, they apologise and we are expected to let them off. There just doesn't seem to be any justice in that and it's no surprise that the young people of today have no respect for either them or other members of the public. Personally I have been a witness to serious crimes committed by what we are supposed to believe are pillars of society, who in any event will rip us off even if it's just a few quid on their parliamentary expenses account. Don't believe for one moment that the money that is being thrown at them for their campaigns is free, remember the saying 'There is nothing free about a free lunch', it always has a price.

Many years ago I had a friend with whom I made and shared a fortune with, I was young and maybe a little bit naive and I have believed that it was much better to enjoy oneself at that time of ones life. I was doing exactly that living life to the full, however my friend was exactly the opposite, he bought a house, he got himself a top of the range car, and like myself he liked an expensive diamond ring, he more or less had everything he had originally wished for. We kept on making money which he invested into a small but successful business. He had a lovely wife and one child, he really did have the lot, as the money rolled in he decided to get a 'safe' in which he secured his money and his diamonds! Apart from going out for the occasional meal with his family he did not risk doing much else especially if that would cause him to spend his money, he soon became known as a 'greedy, tight arse'. He once told me that he was aware that he was gaining a reputation as a greedy man, he certainly did not help himself to get rid of such a reputation.

Johnny was his first name, I found it embarrassing whenever we both visited other friends of mine (non villains included), he would always have a packet of ten cigarettes in his 'very deep pocket' he would then beg cigarettes from my pals who would later say to me, is that the bloke with all the money? To which I would say yes that's him. I would then hear the proverbial chorus of 'the greedy bastard'. The ironic thing was that some of the money which was in his safe came from the millions of cigarettes we nicked from warehouses and cash and carries.

I mention Johnny because he is a good example of a person who is smitten by the terrible affliction and disease known as "greed". When I think of him it makes me wonder what makes people like that and why some people are inclined to be that way. He once confided in me that it did annoy him to know that he was known as a greedy tight arse, he was in denial of it. I remember saying to him, lets put it this way, I think that you have an "extremely frugal disposition" at this he looked rather puzzled, he did not answer; at least I summed him up in a more tactful way than the others normally did. I looked at the wider picture concerning greed, such as big business people, some of whom I have met, some members of parliament, and so on. I then think of an even wider picture which I would describe as global greed. Remember a large percentage of global wealth is in the clutches of an extreme minority, money is power, which is why the United States is the most powerful country in the globe, and then on the flip side there are millions of people dying of hunger, and of poverty, why should this be?

There is more than enough wealth in the world to ensure that all the creatures of this planet can have, or should be able to expect, a decent standard of living. Every person on the planet should be given the right to live their lives with some pride and dignity, but sadly, that is a dream that will never happen due to the murky world of politics and greed. It also comes down to 'human nature', we all feel the need to survive, but for so many people it goes far beyond that human trait to survive, they want it all, they can never be satisfied with what they have, and they achieve their aim to the detriment of millions of others. I wonder if such people have taken the time to consider the *real meaning* of the words "The first one now will later be last"?

In the Geordie Underworld there were some greedy tight arses, but there were a lot more people like me who liked to give a slice of their ill-gotten gains taken from the rich to the people on the breadline who needed it. When I refer to the Geordie Underworld I'm not just talking about so-called villains like me, but also the many corrupt so-called respectable people who found themselves on the wrong side of the law due to their insatiable greed for more money, influence and power.

CHAPTER EIGHTTEEN
THE BIGGEST JOB
IN THE NORTH EAST

THE VILLAINS of the North East and elsewhere who came to my house for a natter on jobs they were planning were always given the best natter I could give them, providing they had come with a recommendation from people that I knew. In the crime game it was always best that the person you were dealing with could be vouched for by someone you knew and trusted. I couldn't give natter, or chat, to just any Tom, Dick or Harry who turned up on my doorstep.

Mario, Joe Camelo, Gladys.

One person who arrived at my house in Newcastle for some natter in 1993 did not need any introductions nor did he need anyone to vouch for him. It was Joe Camelo, a great friend of mine since the 1960s whom I had worked on a lot of jobs with and with whom I had earned a lot of money in the process. Joe was a larger-than-life character, always laughing. He was an affable, personable, man who would do anything he could for friends. It was me who had introduced Joe to the woman who would become his wife, Marcelle.

148

In the living room of my house Joe outlined the job he had in mind, and it turned out to be the biggest job ever carried out in the North East of England at the time worth £9.2million, which was a fortune in 1993. But the size of the job would bring with it sizeable risks.

Joe told me he had gotten a team together which he trusted and they were going to hit a massive social security office in St James' Street, Newcastle, to seize a haul of benefit books and giro cheques, along with documents that would make them difficult to trace, and then distribute them throughout the region to people on the payroll who would cash them for a small percentage.

The office complex Joe was referring too was quite modern, had a very sophisticated alarm system and a top-of-the-range, state-of-the-art safe that would prove a challenge to even the most experienced of safe blowers. That, Joe was hoping, was where I would come in.

I didn't give Joe any natter, I gave him some advice. My advice to Joe was simple, straightforward, and something he didn't want to hear: "Don't do it. It's jailbait," I said.

I told him it wasn't a wise adventure. I told him that once he got the millions of pounds worth of cheques he would then have to employ many people to change them into cash and that there was not many people who could be trusted to keep their traps shut once they were caught. I told him with there being millions of pounds worth of Government assets there would be lots of resources and efforts put in to catching those responsible by the authorities. I knew it would be impossible to get rid of the cheques in one shot as they would be so hot no one in their right minds would touch them. "Someone will grass you up, and you'll end up serving a long time," I told Joe.

Despite my advice, which was freely given to a trusted old friend, a short time later Joe and his team did the job. They employed people to hand ball the cheques to different post offices, then the inevitable happened. A couple of people got caught, then Joe's name was put straight into the frame and serious observations were carried out on him by the police. This ended up with him getting a jail sentence of eight-and-a-half years, during which time he lost his wife to his own brother. In fact he lost everything.

The big burglary happened when he was aged 53 and living in Benton, Newcastle. A 32cwt safe was cracked and inside were giros and benefit books, which had been delivered two days earlier, along with authorisation stamps, inkpads and information that would have helped trace the stolen documents. In the haul 592 cheques worth more than £155,000 were cashed before the gang was caught. A search of a house Joe had access to uncovered a sawn-off shotgun, three ski masks, forged driving licences and three briefcases containing items such as cutting equipment. The Judge in the case against Joe and his team at Newcastle Crown Court, Richard Lowden, said it was perhaps the biggest burglary Tyneside had ever seen.

I had done some good jobs with Joe and had made a lot of money with him. But the bottom line is I have always gone by my own instincts and again I was proved right in the biggest job in the North East. That's why I have never seen the inside of a long-term prison, much to the annoyance of the establishment. They really wanted to lock me up for a long time, but they failed.

Joe did his time and when he came out I kept in regular touch with him. In fact he was the best man at my wedding in 1991, that was how close we were. He and I both retired from the crime game at about this time, but we were both tapped for advice from many of the up-and-coming new faces in the North East underworld.

Joe Camelo & Mario

Sadly, in August 2008, and only three weeks after I had last seen Joe, he hanged himself in the loft of his house in Enslin Street, Walker, in the East End of Newcastle. He had left a suicide note asking for forgiveness from his family and put his action down to "this condition of mine". I was not aware that Joe had suffered from depression for many years. In fact he had been diagnosed with bi-polar disorder, more commonly known as manic depression, where the victim suffers extreme mood swings, from the depths of despair to the heights of elation.

A funeral service for Joe took place at St Anthony's Padua Church, Walker Newcastle, followed by internment at All Saint's Crematorium, Jesmond. From all accounts the service was packed to the rafters. I did not go to his funeral for two reasons. First of all it was too early due to my medical condition but secondly and mainly because I did not want to see his wife, Marcelle, or his brother Michael. It was ironic that I had introduced Marcelle, his wife, to Joe. If I had gone to the funeral I may well have lost it with them, which would not have been respectful to Joe. I know these things happen in families, especially when a person ends up inside, but I couldn't forget the devastating effect it had had on Joe.

I also couldn't forget the traitor, the Judas, who had betrayed Joe following the big job, probably in return for himself getting a cushy sentence or not even being charged at all. In the crime game even paedophiles, the lowest-of-the-low scum by any standards, are not looked upon with as much disdain and hatred as the grass, who informs on their colleagues. Sadly, the old, honourable, rule "thou shalt not grass", is a tradition that is dying out within crime circles. In the 1960s and later it did not need to be mentioned, it went without saying. But these days, with the crime world so dominated by drugs and low-lifes who would snitch for enough cash for a small heroin wrap, there is less honour in not grassing. It's a sad indictment on the society in which we live, where trust is a virtue rarely witnessed.

The grass is one of the biggest concerns for any professional villain. Who can they trust can quite literarily mean who they can trust with their lives and of course with their very freedom. We are all familiar with cases where a one time trusted villain turns against his own people, which often ends in their once good friends ending up being sent to prison for many years. Serious super grasses have been and will no doubt continue to be around to ensure that their former team mates have been jailed for hundreds of years between them. There is never an excuse for such treachery. The reason why they do it is however simple. They do it because they do not want to go to prison themselves, so in order to achieve their aim they go against their comrades; then after they have done their wicked and cowardly deed they slink away, protected by the very system they once hated. If they had done this whilst serving as a soldier during active service in the past they would be taken out and shot for cowardice and more often than not desertion. Luckily the underworld has its own disciplinary code and some of these despicable low lives do ultimately get the 'Full Monty', they pay the ultimate price and I believe its only right that they do.

It is of course a strange thing for a villain to say but when the police or other institutions are found to have committed a serious crime they all close ranks and the mole in their ranks is ostracised. They then issue the old and tested two word statement 'No Comment', this is a tactic that seems to work for them most of the time. Luckily for me I only discovered a 'Judas' in the camp on just a couple of occasions in over a thirty five year career. Yes they did pay the ultimate price, of which I have not got one grain of regret in taking the action that was in any event absolutely necessary. Jesus may have forgiven Judas, but I believe that he must have been a serious and selfish low life who in a sense merely took the view that it was better for him to put all his comrades on the cross or jail, so that he could stay free. In my day there was a strict code amongst proper and genuine villains, a code that appears to be a distant memory to the so called villains of today.

When the drug trade really kicked in within the United Kingdom the whole face of crime went through a dramatic change, out went the strict code of the true genuine villains; the code vanished overnight. The drug trade attracted all kinds of people and most of those people can never be described as real villains, most of them are in fact just ordinary people who find it easy to sell their products quite literarilly from their own doorstep. In some cases these people were obliged to go on the frontline, let's say the pavement or street corner, but then most of them would neither have the bottle or the brain cells to organise a big job, so they often feel that selling drugs is the best deal for them. And as we are all well aware by now the drugs trade is absolutely littered with informants. This obviously goes a long way to explain why there is now a population of eighty thousand people in prison, this is a statistic that has almost doubled since the drug trade took root in the United Kingdom.

I have, throughout the years, often been invited by my many contacts to come in and enter the world of narcotics, always and without any hesitation I have refused point blank to get involved in this murky world. I probably could have made another fortune in that game, but it was definitely not for me. Crack cocaine is a drug that I personally had problems with, but I had the strength to go cold turkey as they call it and beat it. Another reason why I would not go into the drugs trade is that it is a business where people have to put their face up front to all kinds of unknown and untested people. When I was doing my own thing I would often do all the homework on my own, no one knew what I was planning and I made sure that nothing was left around for them to even guess that I might be planning something.

I had in effect the advantage to catch the target completely by surprise and without any warning. I could always keep my secret to myself, then once the target was caught by surprise and off guard I could then simply slip away saying nothing to anyone. I always felt safe and secure with my own way of doing things and I could simply always trust myself. Even the original Mafia have themselves been victims of traitors, those within their ranks who could be persuaded to turn against their friends and colleagues. I never wanted to be part of a gang and I know that people believe in the old saying of 'safety in numbers', but I personally feel that it is completely the reverse of this, it is indeed far less secure and definitely not safe to have so many know your business. When other people know all or most of your business the chances are that even more will find out. My code on this has served me well and I always say that the less anyone knows about your business the more chance you have of carrying it out without getting caught. I often remember the old code of conduct used by the navy: "loose lips sink ships".

CHAPTER NINETEEN
THE BURNING RING OF FIRE

THE NIGHT that Tyneside erupted in violence and flames may have been sparked by the deaths of two local youths who crashed a stolen car at speed whilst being chased by police but the fuel that fanned the flames had been there for decades in the deep resentment felt by local people against the authorities, particularly the police. The people on the Meadow Well estate in North Tyneside were labelled the "underclass" and the police reaction against any trouble had always been to move in hard and quick to extinguish the trouble, much like firefighters would tackle a car blaze.

The Meadow Well Riots broke out in September 1991 on the large council housing estate, east of Newcastle, which was formerly known as The Ridges, a name the authorities changed to Meadow Well in a desk-bound public relations exercise to rid the area of its reputation for crime and anti-social behaviour. It didn't work.

The estate was built in the 1930s to house families on low income from nearby North Shields. By the late 1980s and just before the riots, the estate was considered a no go area for many people from the outside and for the police. Seeing a police officer on the beat was as rare as seeing a Sunderland fan in his home football shirt on the terraces of the Gallowgate end in the old St James' Park. The *underclass* on the Meadow Well estate, like those living on many other run-down council estates in the UK where riots also broke out at about the same time, had been ignored by the authorities for decades and demonised by the middle-class members of the Press who rarely ventured out of their ivory-towered offices to see what life was really like on the streets of Britain. But the media were out in force on the nights of the riots and Tyneside remained in the national headlines for many weeks.

The riots were triggered by the deaths of local youths, Dale Robson and Colin Atkins, who were killed whilst driving a stolen motor car which was being pursued at high speed by the police. Friends of the pair claimed on local news broadcasts that their deaths were caused by the police forcing their vehicle from the road. On the first nights of the riots, when Meadow Well really did become a no-go area, locals looted shops and set buildings on fire, including a youth centre, a fish and chip shop, and an electricity sub-station. Police and fire crews which attended the scene were pelted with bricks, as were those outsiders who the rioters believed may have been members of Her Majesty's Press. It was estimated that at its height 400 people were involved in the troubles. Lines of police officers in full riot gear eventually moved in and the Northumbria Police helicopter hovered overhead, its strong beam of light shining on the rioters below who were shielding their faces with scarves. The riots continued for a few days, and spread to the West End of Newcastle and Scotswood.

For me this was not just a bunch of young thugs making the most of an opportunity to loot and have a go at the bizzies, it was the dawn of a local revolution which would send the strongest message out possible to those in authority that they had to take notice. That people were sick of living in squalor; sick of being ignored; sick of not being given any opportunities whilst those around them prospered and sick of being branded the "underclass". Yes, not the "working class" which they were, if they could find work, but the "underclass", the lowest-of-the-low in our class-ridden society where the few enjoy wealth and privilege, usually inherited, the majority live in middle-class comfort and the minority are left to rot in a shithole, the rest would say, of their own making.

The Meadow Well Riots inspired me to pick up a pen and paper and my guitar and write a song titled "*It's Not Your Destiny*".

Down on your knees, they want you to be
For you there's only poverty
It's not you fault, as they well know
They say it's your fate, your destiny

The better life is there for you to see
It's out of your reach, for you there's only misery
Some have it all, more than they need
Driven on by selfishness, driven on by greed

THE GEORDIE GODFATHER

They tell you there's plenty, you know that is true
Plenty for them but nothing for you
The politician, the rich man, looks down on you
Take your jobs while you join the queue

You look at your children, on how can I cope?
Their eyes tell their story, no future, no hope
Your home is the ghetto, is there no escape?
You think of your neighbour, whose own life he did take

You try to stay clean, like you've always been
You don't have much choice, do you fade or do you steal?

Chorus

Wake up people, can't you see?
It's not your fate
It's not your destiny

The politician he said 'I've got news for you'
We're building more prisons, to make room for you
The riots, the crime, they say it's a shame
While they live in style, and you have the pain

Think of the father, rotting in jail
And of his children who stand in the rain
Think of the mother, whose son dies in jail
She gets no answers, just lies and more pain

People don't like us, that's their cry
"Anti-police" and they all wonder why
Birmingham Six, Guildford Four
Winston Silcott and many more

Police corruption, disband the force
Perjured evidence and lies galore
Forensic science is corrupt as well
Innocent people living in Hell

Took to the Station alive and well
Out in a coffin, killed by them
Close ranks, close ranks, can't tell the truth
Cover it up like they always do

Round the table, compare their notes
Word for word, no reproach
They jail the innocent and have no regret
Then wonder why the young have no respect

The Judge in the court with wealth and degrees
Sends you down saying 'next one please'
He has no thought for those you leave behind
More struggle and strife from your heartbroken wife

They brand you a bad man, for the rest of your life
But you know and I know it's you that is right
For they are the criminals for the crimes against you
Crimes against the people, but they punish you

They don't have to worry, if you complain
Enquiry team are just the same
Got it made when they commit crime
The systems behind them all of the time

Chorus

Wake up you people, can't you see
It's not your fate, it's not your destiny

A few bad apples is what they say
More lies and propaganda coming your way
Don't they realise what they do?
If they lock up the poor, the family suffers too

Your kids see it all, it's not what they thought
Great British justice, that's what they were taught
You look around you and think how they dare?
You know you're the victim, you know they don't care

Just think of yourself, that's how they play the game
Or get left behind in poverty and pain
I've got a solution, say they with it all
Lock them away while we have a ball

A new generation had better take heed
For the young see right through their power and greed
People please listen, listen to me
Don't let them keep you in misery

So just beware that the forces of law
Don't come knocking upon your door
Get off your knees and fight for your cause
Don't let them beat you, don't take anymore

Chorus

Wake up you people, can't you see
It's not your fate, it's not your destiny

Meadow Well, Meadow Well, how do you do?
Sure hope things improve for you

Chorus

Wake up you people, can't you see
It's not your fate, it's not your destiny

It didn't take me long to write the song, as I was so passionate about the message it contained. I recorded it on a few CDs and it was soon circulating all across Tyneside, listened to by hundreds of people. I was told it had become a bit of an underground hit!

But imagine my surprise when the bizzies knocked on my door to talk to me about the recording. They said I could be done for attempting to incite a riot! What a bloody liberty. Whatever happened to free speech. I couldn't imagine them knocking on Bob Dylan's door or the door of Bob Marley, who wrote many songs of protest. I asked the bizzies if they didn't have better things to do. After a few minutes they left. I wasn't cautioned or arrested. I was just amazed.

Since the Meadow Well riots, £66 million has been spent on regenerating the estate. About 750 properties have been demolished and new houses have been built. A new community centre, health centre, and police station have also been built. The total cost of policing the Riots was £7.5million. If the authorities had spent that much on the estate before the riots, there wouldn't have been any bloody riots!

There were more than 300 people arrested in the North East during the disturbances - three times more than any other UK force in that troubled period. At the time of the riots, Northumbria Police had the worst crime rate in the country. Every year the crime rate has successively gone down, down, down and the police say we can all now feel safer on the streets and in our own homes. Really?

If the Meadow Well Riots proved anything, it was that if you rise up in sufficient numbers and protest against injustice and take a hard stand against the authorities, then the authorities have to take notice. (But believe me I am not attempting to incite riots here, I am just making a point).

I used to write songs when I was in prison and I still take up my guitar from time to time. Some people have compared my voice and the words of the songs that I write to those of Johnny Cash. I suppose that's down to doing a bit of time, but who knows?

CHAPTER TWENTY
LAZARUS – A FRIEND IN NEED

AS darkness fell I stood outside what looked like an 18th Century mansion, carrying nothing more than a holdall with a few clothes inside, as if I had just approached a guest house in a strange town and was looking to see if they had any vacancies for the night. But the house was owned by a very successful charity run by a very good friend of mine, George Craig, and I was there for a reason, looking for solitude to get me away from the temptations that had surrounded me for many years and had plunged me into the depths of despair. The temptations were to do with drugs.

In the 1960s pills were all around us, uppers and downers, blueys, purple hearts, and I had tried them all, along with the regular spliff of hashish, but I could take them or leave them. I had never become addicted. In the 1970s and 1980s the drugs were just as easily available, only their names had changed, speed (amphetamine sulphate), Ecstacy and heroin in all its forms from cheap brown to more purer quality smack that had led to the downfall of so many people. In the later years my drug of choice was cocaine, at one time considered the drug of the rich and famous but which had become so freely available and cheap that anyone could afford a gram.

My cocaine use was not so much recreational as medicinal, as it gave me relief from the chronic pain and tiredness of the illness I had been diagnosed with, myalgic encephamyilitis (ME) more commonly known as *yuppie flu* in the 1990s. But ME was not confined to the so-called young and upwardly mobile trendsetters, it could be contracted by anyone from any walk of life, as I discovered to my own cost. There were days when I could not get out of bed; the phone would ring, people would knock on the door, and I would ignore them all, pulling the duvet over my head whilst seeking the comfort of relaxation and the peace of being alone. The chronic tiredness I felt, and still do most afternoons, is really indescribable and only people who have suffered this illness can really understand it.

What compounded the condition for me was the slight brain damage I had suffered years earlier when I fell over in a pub in Newcastle's Bigg Market. Many hospital tests had been done on me and over the years I had been given many different prescribed drugs to alleviate the pain and tiredness. The pain relief was always short lived. There was no magic solution for me and no such thing as a cure. So I sought a release from the pain in any way I could. At first it was a few pints, but that would only leave me bloated and with a hangover the following morning. Then it was cannabis, which I enjoyed; it gave me a sense of well-being, but still left me with no energy. Then along came Charlie, and I was thrown head-first into a whole new world. My first few lines came as a welcome relief from the pain and tiredness – the last time I had felt so energetic was when I was in my twenties. The feel good buzz was phenomenal and I could do things physically with more exertion and more staying power than ever. But what really got me hooked was the mental agility the drug gave me. With alcohol, apparently, the drinker can sometimes get what is called a *moment of clarity*, but cocaine, for me, made everything as clear as day, all day, if I took enough of the stuff. I began playing the guitar and writing songs again and the lyrics were so deep, so profound and so meaningful the young up-and-coming faces on Tyneside who heard my songs, referred to me, probably tongue in cheek, as the Geordie Bob Dylan.

With all my contacts in the Geordie underworld good cocaine, and I'm talking about the pure stuff which isn't mixed with baking powder, flour or talcum powder, was coming to me rather than me having to go to it. It was easier getting hold of it than even getting the prescription drugs I had been relying upon. At least I didn't have to ask for a repeat prescription, which would mean waiting for up to two days and getting someone to go to the GP's surgery to collect it for me. My new drugs came to my door within minutes of asking for them, and the escape into my new, exciting, clear-thinking world came as quickly as the pure powder travelled up my nostrils through the crisp, rolled-up twenty pound note that funnelled it into my brain. I was snorting so much of the white stuff that I once looked like Al Pacino in the film Scarface when he had a mountain of it on a table in front of him. All right, perhaps that's a bit of an exaggeration, but I was at least going through a molehill of the stuff every day, and that's a lot of cocaine. Have you seen the size of those molehills?

A little of what you fancy does you good, goes without saying, but a lot of what you really fancy, we all know, eventually does you more harm than good. My doctor, whom I went to see about my ME, had noted my increased blood pressure, the dilated pupils in my eyes. He seemed worried and asked me if I was eating well. The truth was I didn't really want to eat. I had lost a lot of weight, granted, but I didn't feel weak. It was only after a thorough medical examination by him, and a few home truths from myself, that he warned me I faced major medical complications and health problems, from heart disease, heart attacks, respiratory failure, strokes, seizures, and stomach problems, on the more serious side, to convulsions, nausea, blurred vision, chest pain, fever, and muscle spasms as the minor effects, and that was only on the physical side. On the mental health side he told me my cocaine use could also lead to paranoia, hallucinations and violent mood swings. I had been wondering what that elephant had been doing in my living room the other night, why he seemed to have it in for me, and why the hell I took a swing at him with the hose from my vacuum cleaner. It was only when the doctor told me if I continued on the slippery slope I was on it was inevitable I would end up in a drug-induced coma leading to my death.

That was my wake-up call, and the call that found me, holdall in hand, knocking on the door at Doxford House in the Warden Law area of Sunderland where my old friend George Craig ran the most successful drug rehabilitation and alcohol detoxification centre in the North of England. It wasn't The Priory, where all the addict celebrities go, but who needed The Priory when I had the best centre in the North just about on my own doorstep (it was only ten miles from Newcastle) run by one of my closest friends.

There were a few lights on on the first floor of the building where the bedrooms, I later learned, for those in residential care, stayed, and as I knocked on the door again I wondered if it was ever going to be opened. I waited a minute or so, looking through the window of the main entrance door into the hallway inside, then a small chap with long hair, who looked like a remnant from the hippy sixties, came walking down the ornate staircase with a mug of tea in one hand and a file in the other. He appeared apprehensive as he looked through the window at me, and gingerly unlocked the door, which was opened slowly with a creak.

"Hello," said the man. "Can I help you?"

"Hello, I'm Mario," I said. "Sorry to land up on your doorstep but I'm a friend of George's. Is he in?"

"He left about an hour ago," said the man, looking me over and sussing me out. "How do you know George?"

"We go back a very long time," I said. "We served time together in Durham Jail. I only saw him about three months ago."

The man asked if I would wait a while in the foyer while he rang George. Moments later he reappeared with a smile on his face and asked me to follow him upstairs to one of the dining rooms.

"George is on his way," he said. "Told me to show you some hospitality while you wait. My name's Jeremy by the way." The man put out his hand and I shook it firmly, then we walked along a corridor, with bedrooms either side. One man was standing at a bedroom door. He just stared, not suspiciously, more enquiringly and not in an unfriendly way.

Minutes earlier, walking across the marble-floored foyer, which had an impressive fountain with a cherub spouting water in one corner, and then being led up the magnificent, oak-panelled stairway of what was this grand mansion house, I have to say I was greatly impressed. The floodlights were on at the rear of the house and through a window I could just see the outline of many trees covering several acres and what looked like a stream running through the grounds.

I took a seat at a fine table in the dining room and Jeremy entered with a plate of sandwiches and cold soft drink.

"That's great," I said. "But could I have a nice cup of tea rather than the soft drink?"

"No problem," said Jeremy and he moved back into the adjoining kitchen to the put the kettle on.

"This is a fantastic house," I said.

"What was that," said Jeremy, appearing at the kitchen doorway.

"Sorry, I couldn't hear you for the kettle."

"Great house," I said. "Just fantastic."

"Used to belong to a well-known shipbuilding family in Sunderland, the Doxfords," Jeremy said. "It's got a fascinating history. It was just about derelict when we took it over."

"Must have cost a bomb," I said.

"About a million."

"Bloody hell! Where did George get that kind of money?" I asked surprised.

"From people who believe in him, and believe in what he's doing."

I had heard from many people that George Craig, a one-time robber, who had turned his back on crime and hadn't had his collar felt for more than twenty years, but I was amazed and just as equally impressed with the success of the charity – the Lazarus Foundation – he had built up from nothing, . It was named after the character from the bible who was brought back to life, given a second chance, just like George and his team were giving to many people who could have otherwise ended up in the gutter with a dirty needle in their arm or on a cold mortuary slab.

As I could feel the shakes coming on me, after only three or so hours since my last fix, and shivers starting to run through my body, Jeremy told me about the huge obstacles that had been placed in George's way trying to build up the Lazarus charity. I listened, but in my haze some of it was lost on me. George and I had done some bits of work during his criminal career, which hadn't lasted that long, and those jobs had been hugely profitable, and he had genuinely wanted to put the past behind him, but once you're labelled a criminal by the authorities it is almost impossible to shake that branding off. His charity had started off, Jeremy told me, in a small office in Sunderland's Norfolk Street, providing meals and clothing to those in need and counselling for addicts trying to shake their habits. Many of these downtrodden people, neglected by the state that was supposed to provide for them, often wanted no more than a cup of tea and a friendly chat, and George and his small band of unpaid volunteers, were happy just to sit and listen. The cash for Doxford House came from a religious organisation with no ties to the state, and there was a paper trail to prove it, but the authorities, particularly the local police, hated George and resented the fact that he was making a success of his charity despite the barriers placed in his way. It wasn't long before he, his lovely wife Denise, and Jeremy all had their collars felt on some trumped up charges which were never proven. The charges could never have been proven, because there had not been any criminal offences committed. But that's what life is like for someone who has served time. The authorities never want to forget it. No wonder that George Craig titled his life story *Mud Sticks*, the fella has had bucket-loads of mud flung his way, but he rises above it, just like Lazarus rose from the dead. I suppose George saw the charity as him giving something back to the community; saw it as his second chance.

As Jeremy spoke of the charity's trials and tribulations my larger-than-life friend, with a smile beaming from his face, arrived at the dining room door, after having climbed the stairs. For a big fella, he was quite fit. He shook me by the hand and embraced me like an old and trusted friend would.

"Why didn't you phone me?" He asked.

"I lost your number," was my slightly pathetic excuse.

Then we got down to the brass tacks, a trait I had always admired in George. What had brought me to Doxford House in Sunderland on a cold November night, with a gaunt-looking face, ashen skin, a small holdall and a worried expression? I told George all about it and, as I would have expected, he was sympathetic and said he would do anything he could to help me. He told me about the detoxification services his charity offered, the pioneering 12-steps programme to recovery, the counselling available and other services, and he would be offering them without asking for a penny in return.

"All I want is for you to put me in a room with a sink, a toilet, a shower and a bed and two weeks' worth of food and water," I said.

"You don't have to do that, you daft bugger," George said. "We've got professional people here, trained people, who can help you."

"Thanks, but I really want, I really need to do this myself," I said. "I need to do it cold turkey. I know I can do it, if I'm away from temptation."

"Well you'll not find any drugs here," said George. "Except for maybe a few aspirins. You always were a single-minded sod. Always liked to do things your own way."

This was true. George knew me very well and he knew that when I said I was going to do something, I would do it.

After a couple of cups of tea, a sandwich or two and a good natter, George showed me to an en-suite room on the first floor of the mansion house. I didn't sleep at all that first night because I was shaking uncontrollably. The first few days passed and the hallucinations, headaches and foaming from the mouth gradually subsided. For two weeks I stayed in that one room, in my own private hell on earth. And in those long moments of self-enforced solitary confinement I found the inner-strength to see me through. I am not a religious man, all that was knocked out of me during my nightmarish time in the orphanage, but when I left Doxford House, saying goodbye to George and Jeremy, I knew I had vanquished my demons and, like Lazarus, it seemed I had risen from the dead.

George later went on to open a centre for recovering alcoholics and drug addicts in the centre of Sunderland and later a community cafe, named George's Community Cafe in recognition of all the work he had done in the local community and rightly deserved, on the north side of the city's River Wear. Again for people who were in need of help and for whom the authorities, the social services and the like, had resoundingly failed to support. There's an old saying that a friend in need is a friend in deed. I was the friend in need and George proved beyond any doubt that it is when you are at your lowest ebb in life that you really find out who your true friends are. I am proud to still count him amongst my very best friends.

CHAPTER TWENTY ONE

MY BROTHER

I moved in with a woman in a house in Lancashire and Preston was a nice place. I wasn't there long when one day at the local football match I bumped into an old pal from Newcastle. He told me that my brother Michael was seriously ill and as a result I hot footed it back to Newcastle to see him. I was on my toes at the time but getting caught didn't come in to it. Michael was my brother and if he was ill, no matter what, I was going to see him.

Back in Newcastle I immediately went to see Michael in the Newcastle General Hospital. I knew that going back to Newcastle, where so many people knew me was taking a big chance, but Michael was my brother and it was more important to be there for him, than to be free on the outside. Ok, I might get caught, but to be honest I was not too worried about that, as I had achieved more than I had escaped Durham

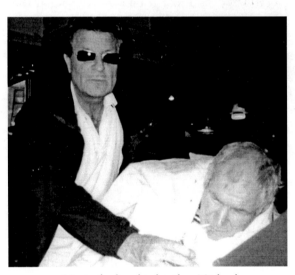

Mario feeding his brother Michael not long before he died.

Prison for in the first place. I was well connected, had money, smart suits and a nice car, but to be there for Michael was in any event more important to me. Anyway I got the chance to see Michael, who had just had a cancerous tumour removed from his brain; this was destined to leave him seriously disabled for the rest of his life. I then went to see my other brothers and sisters at 'mothers', with the intention of moving on in a day or two. After

167

a couple of days I was saying goodbye to them and, having packed my bag, was about to leave and move on, but within seconds the house was surrounded by police. There were that many of them you would think that I was a serial killer and not just a villain. Anyway I decided to give myself up, as any other course of action would only end up with the same result. I remember one of them saying that they were terrified that I was going to come out fighting and that I had done the right thing.

The situation with my brother made me remember what we got

Sister Maureen.

up to in our younger days. I remembered a relation telling me, for I was on the run at the time, that Michael came home one day and was up a height. He had just got a job working at the Delta Works in Lemington. It was an extremely dirty job though and very hard work. However this turned out to be just another one of life's dirty tricks, he was working there and had an accident when a crane hook hit him, knocking him on the side of the head. Sadly our Michael was never the same again. It was 1965 and he took poorly the day I got married and he became progressively worse in hospitals and homes until the day he died.

Anything bad that I have endured during my life pales into insignificance to that of the life of my brother Michael. We all tend to use the word tragic, but Michael's life from the beginning to the end was indeed one enormous tragedy. Like myself, Michael was taken into care, he was only eighteen months old when, after being found in an appalling condition suffering from both malnutrition and serious neglect, he was thrust into the system. I was already in care at St Mary's Orphanage or home in Tudhoe. I remember clearly that when I was about four years old being called over by a Nun who was holding a child in her arms. The Nun said "Do you know who this is?" I do not remember if I replied, but I do remember her saying "This is your brother Michael".

I was then moved on from the nursery to the juniors section which was in another part of the building, which explains why I do not recall hardly anything about Michael in that terrible place. It was not until years later that I learned that Michael had then been taken from the Orphanage and was placed back with his mother: (This was a tragic and very bad mistake). A mother who had not changed one bit from when we were taken from her. He was then only about thirteen or fourteen years old. I have since learned that he was treated very badly by the mother that he did not really know. My sister Maureen told me that he was a lovely lad, but he was treated like a slave, at the age of 19 he was taken bad and ended up having an operation to remove a cancerous tumour.

Daughter Norma, son in law Smidda & pal Eddie Carlisle.

This operation left him with a disability that was to get progressively worse as the years went on. In the last fifteen to twenty years of his life, he was unable to move, unable to talk and was in terrible pain, it really was a nightmare seeing him suffer like that, after visiting him I would leave him with a heavy heart. I would be frustrated at being unable to help him to erase any of the pain, although he could not talk his eyes told me of the suffering he was going through. I can clearly remember that I would take great joy in sometimes getting a small smile from Michael; he really was a brave human being. I have never known anyone who has suffered so much and for so long, surely no one, but no one, should have to bear such suffering, especially a lovely person who everyone knew Michael was. The God who he had been forced to have faith in had without doubt abandoned him, it was indeed the worst tragedy I have ever witnessed, and we all often ask the question why should certain people suffer so much in their lives? I feel that there is no answer to this, it is merely fate that had dealt such a horrendous affliction on Michael, and the way I see it is that there is just no logic to it.

Michael died with family members at his bedside at the age of fifty eight years old and to be perfectly honest I was both extremely sad and also relieved at the same time. Sad because I had lost part of me, as my mind goes back to those words in 1945 when the Nun said to me "Do you know who this is?", words that have been imbedded deep in my mind since the day they were first unceremoniously uttered. I also felt relieved and comforted in the knowledge that at last Michael was 'free' from the pain and frustration. In Michael's case it was really a case befitting the words "In some extreme circumstances, death can indeed be a release from the pain of life".

Michael's death effected me in a very profound way, also in a very private way, but sadly still I was unable to cry. That cannot be normal, but I try and reassure myself by telling myself that one does not have to shed tears to be genuinely sad and effected at the loss of a remarkable man like Michael. There is also such a thing as false tears of which I can never be accused. Wherever Michael may be, he and I know how we both feel and that is good enough for me.

CHAPTER TWENTY TWO
MY SISTERS & BROTHERS

Although my childhood was bad enough the one endured by my brothers and sisters was just as bad. My sister was relating her experiences to me and I could not leave these out from this book. My sister Maureen went to see the priest and in her own words I quote what the priest said "I can't find anyone baptized by the name of Renwick", he said "I have looked through all the records at the English Martyrs Church". Maureen then went home and told her mother and she just said "Well try Cunningham", it is really sad, when all Maureen needed was a copy of her birth certificate so that she could be married in a Catholic Church. The year was 1965 and Maureen was 18 years old.

She then went on to tell me that her first memory is sitting on a step on Westmorland Road in Newcastle, whilst her mother was giving birth. The next thing she remembered was being told that the baby had died. Shortly after this they all moved to Blakelaw, that was Maureen and her mother and father. A few years later she remembered her two brothers coming into the world and also living in the new council house in Blakelaw. This house had a bathroom, but her mother just could not settle there and often used to drift back to the bars and people that she knew down Westmorland Road. Mother was again drinking heavy and staying out. Maureen told me that dad used to take the boys and her down to the bars and ask her mother to come home, but she would just say that she would be back shortly, but sometimes they wouldn't see her for days. Maureen says that her dad was always there and didn't leave them, we didn't have much money and things were tight, but somehow mother always found a 'set in' for a drink.

Maureen said mother would often come home really drunk, sometimes with the rough people from the bars that she frequented and there would be fighting. They used to dread mother coming home and would often lay awake listening to it all. She would sometimes hit dad, but she did not hit the bairns. Maureen said they never had any clocks in the house because mother would come home and throw a clock at the wall in her

171

drunken tempers; lamps were another thing that went down the swanny! Mother did not drink in the house, but went out most nights. Dad had a bad chest and used to be hospitalised or in the sanatorium, but mother still went out. Maureen stayed with the young ones, but they were free to do as they liked. Maureen said she was aware she had two brothers and a sister, but never met them. Mother used to mention them and Maureen said she thought she had visited myself and Michael at Tudhoe Home, but never Margaret who at that time was in Birmingham. Michael came back to Maureen's house when he was 14 years old and at first he went to school. He then worked in the dairy and he played football for them, he loved his football. Michael was a quiet mild mannered young man, one who if met would leave a lasting impression on you, he also had a very lovely nature, we got on so well and used to go 'bopping' (dancing).

Mario's son John on holiday

Maureen said both Margaret and me were not on the scene then. Mother was still drinking heavily and causing lot's of trouble, out drinking until late and bringing rough strangers back to the house at night. Maureen said she met Margaret when she was sent back to Newcastle for about five months, but then she went away again. When I was 17 years old I was brought back to the house by the priest, and Maureen remembered this. I had just got work at British Rail delivering parcels. Michael at this time was still at school. Maureen remembered that I was shocked at mother's drinking as I had not seen anything like that before. Maureen used to practice 'bopping' and I loved dancing too. I was going out with

172

a lass called Norma, then I worked delivering coal and then in the building of English Martyrs, but by this time mother was taking me down the bars in Marlborough showing me a life I had never seen before. Mother used to like to show us off. Margaret came back home when she was around 16 years of age from the 'Good Shepherd' and she and Maureen became good friends straight away, and have remained good friends to this day. Margaret didn't stay long as mother was still up to her old antics: coming in fighting and arguing with all of them through drink. Margaret had not seen anything like that and didn't want to stay and she left after enduring it for about nine months. I also left after that. So it was Michael, Robert, Frankie and Maureen that were left there.

About five years before she died my mother lived in a small bungalow in the West End of Newcastle upon Tyne; she lived with her then partner Mick Kelly. The thing I remember most was that the place had a ghastly smell. I received a phone call from one of my family asking me to call into the bungalow because Mick was very ill, he had not ate or drank anything for many days. When I got there the smell was even worse than it had ever been, I saw Mick who was lying in bed, he looked shocking, he had a big long beard, he was absolutely filthy, his nails were long and black and he was very thin. He reminded me of a caveman. I could see that this man was dying, I could see fear and shock in his eyes, his mouth and lips were dry.

I turned to my mother who was sitting in the living room with a cup of tea, the television was on. I asked her how long had Mick been in that terrible state, she just looked up and said "oh about a couple of weeks". I think I immediately called an ambulance. Mick realised what was happening and he said, in a very weak voice "just leave me here". He didn't want to move, he was just waiting to die. The ambulance arrived and I picked him up in my arms and carried him to the ambulance. I told my mother to get into the ambulance which then took us to hospital. I went to see him a couple of times after that, they scrubbed him down, cutting his nails etc. I never saw him again and I was told he had died shortly after. I mention the above to give yet another example, another insight into the mindset of my mother Eileen Cunningham. Mick Kelly, but for my intervention, would have died in a filthy and literally not fit for a dog place.

It appears that my mother had done a full circle as my mind

goes back to 1942, by now my mother was well in her seventies. She had not changed, she was without shame, feelings, conscience, without pity, she was just not normal. For a human being to be without such feelings leaves me with no doubt that Eileen Cunningham was seriously ill, there was not just a screw missing, there were *many*. I believe she was incapable of showing any of these normal feelings, simply because she did not have such feelings within her makeup.

I remember she had a dog called Rex at the bungalow which she appeared to like a lot, but yes you've guessed it she couldn't even look after the dog properly. We must therefore assume that she got the dog with the intention of keeping it and looking after it, but she was incapable of doing so. I am now even more convinced that Eileen Cunningham was indeed seriously mentally ill and it was just pure fate and circumstance that dictated that myself and the other surviving members of my family were doomed to be delivered from the womb of such a mother, who herself was obviously born into this world with no feelings in her entire body.

AUCKLAND CHRONICLE, THURSDAY, 2 APRIL 1942

NEWS FROM THE COURTS

Bishop Auckland: Thursday

YOUNG PARENTS SENT TO PRISON

A young South Church couple were charged with neglecting a four month old child. They were Peter Cunningham (26), 2, Peases Street, South Church, and his wife, Ellen (23), of the same address. The husband pleaded "Not Guilty" and the wife "Guilty".

Prosecuting on behalf of the National Society for the Prevention of Cruelty to Children, Mr. E. B. Proud said that the couple had been under observation for some time. It was alleged that the defendants jointly neglected the baby in such a way as to cause injury to health. In 1940 there was some trouble with the defendants relating to children, one an illegitimate child of the woman, and the other an infant. The elder child was sent to Dr. Barnardo's Home and the baby died on admission to Bishop Auckland Poor Law Institution. It was then questionable whether the couple should be prosecuted, but the Society decided not to.

Sergt. Armstrong said the child was left with Mrs. Cunningham, Sen., and she told him that she did not want it. The mother, she said had left the baby 24 hours before and had not returned. He saw the baby in the pram and it was in a filthy condition.

In the pram with the baby were a lot of blacking tins, an empty bottle and some tins on which the baby was lying.

P.C. Youll said the house was in a filthy condition.

Not Fit for a Dog

Inspector Ellwood, N.S.P.C.C., said the male defendant told him that his wife had left him and he had taken the baby to his mother's home. The condition in which the child was found was not fit for a dog.

He also corroborated the statements about the state of the defendant's home. He had previously warned the woman. So far as the man was concerned he was living on unemployment assistance of 35s. per week. He had had jobs but would not stay at work.

Describing the case as a disgraceful one, the magistrates decided to send both defendants to prison for six months with hard labour.

I do not really know what to say about my father. I did not know him at all, and I have been told by people who knew him that he was a nice man, that he was a devoted Catholic who followed the doctrine of his faith. He was an Irish man and he was said to be of small stature and height. All I can say is that this nice man was sent to prison twice along with my mother Eileen. The records show that the authorities had discovered a dead baby in the house he shared with my mother. The circumstances in which the baby was found was such that the authorities were considering prosecution for both of them. The piece from the paper when they were both sent to prison for neglecting me states that the infant had died on admission to the institution, yet again the papers had got it wrong. On obtaining the actual death certificate and the coroners report it clearly states that the child was found dead at the mother and father's house.

FD 248!

CERTIFIED COPY
Pursuant to the Births and

of an ENTRY
Deaths Registration Act 1953

				Registration District Durham Western				
1941.	**Death in the Sub-district of** Bishop Auckland				**In the County of** Durham			
Columns:-	1	2	3	4	5	6	7	8	9
No.	When and where died	Name and surname	Sex	Age	Occupation	Cause of death	Signature, description and residence of informant	When registered	Signature of re
8	Twenty Fourth March 1941 Oaklands Bishop Auckland U.D.	Mary Catherine Cunningham	Female	5 Months	of 1 Quarry Houses Westerton Bishop Auckland U.D. Daughter of Peter Aloysius Cunningham General Labourer	1a. Acute Bronchitis Certified by John A. Gaites MB	P.A. Cunningham Father In Attendance 1 Quarry Houses Westerton	Twenty Sixth March 1941	T.D. Bird Registrar

Certified to be a true copy of an entry in a register in my custody.

J.A. Ramage Deputy Superintendent

27.02.2008

Had that child survived she would have been my elder sister, her name was Cathleen. All I can say about the above situation is that the causes of her death were consistent with neglect and compounded by the fact that an elder brother was taken from them and put into care. This makes it clear that something serious had occurred and for some unknown reason they were never prosecuted. This was a bad mistake. There should have been systems in place to prevent further suffering of children, but as it turned out I was to be the next victim of these people. I feel that I may well have suffered the same fate as Cathleen if I had not been taken away from them when I was four months old. Then following me my sister Margaret, and then my brother Michael were found in a dreadful condition.

Both Margaret and Michael were taken into care then amazingly my mother was then free to go on and have more children. She had not changed, she would leave the children for days on end in the care of the father whose chronic illness caused him to spend lengthy periods in a sanatorium. She still stayed away when the father was in hospital, which left my sister Maureen, who was herself only a child of ten, to look after her two brothers. One of the brothers would sometimes be looked after by a neighbour until mother decided to reappear and come home from the pubs, often with men that she had met. I often ask myself how on earth did she get away with it, she had been by then in prison twice, everyone knew she had not changed, what were the authorities doing. She was a serial neglecter of children and yet no one bothered to keep her under some sort of observation or supervision. It beggars belief. Did another child have to die before anything was done? In effect the system failed Maureen and my two younger brothers. It was just pure luck that our Maureen prevented another tragedy.

Despite all the above the remarkable and almost unbelievable thing is I can't remember shedding a tear. Many of the boys in the orphanage did. I often ask myself why was this. I was obviously a very sad and confused child. I just cannot understand why I could not cry, surely it's not normal to go through such a nightmare without shedding a tear. I would love it if someone out there could give me an explanation to this question which is often on my mind even to this day. Am I abnormal, it does cross my mind how ironical it would be for me to inherit so obvious a trait of my mother. The mind boggles, the mysteries and intrigues of life are strange indeed, but unlike mother I am incapable of causing such suffering to children. I sometimes wonder what makes a mother like mine the way she was. What was her childhood like? Why did she show no emotion or indeed any feelings? She certainly did not have a grain of maternal instincts or feelings which come to normal mothers.

Surely it's instinctive, it is abnormal for a mother to be without such normal instincts – to be abnormal means to be different from the norm. I wonder what caused her to be so far removed from what should have come naturally. I can only presume that if she had the wherewithal to be a good mother she would have been exactly that. Any normal woman would not want the stigma of being seen as a bad mother to her offspring, let alone going to prison on two separate occasions having to be put on protection from all the people who naturally despise such women – those who are found guilty of such cruelty and serious neglect to their own defenceless offspring.

The question I ask myself is what was my mother guilty of? Was it indeed merely abnormal behaviour or was she quite simply mentally ill, or was she just a downright wicked person? The answer to this is, I just don't know the answer. Though I would be inclined to think she was mentally ill, in a *very bad* way.

* *

Only a few years ago I bumped into one of the St Mary's Home Old Boys, John Killeen, and his memories of the orphanage, like in my case, had stayed with him all these years. His painful memories of the place came out in a torrent.

St.Mary's Homes – Tudhoe Village c. 1950

He said: "I am two people and I have two names, although I was born John Brian Killeen, my other name is number eight, like Mario or number nine, we were for many years, merely a number. The nuns or the Sisters of Charity always called us by our number, we were never referred to by our names. I often consider this when I hear accounts of the concentration camps that existed during the early years that I spent in our hell, Tudhoe Home or Orphanage. We, like those that suffered there were not considered human, we were sinners, we were nothing more than a number. The evil people never told a child that they had a brother in this place, they would never let us know anything, and they told us nothing. I remember one poor sod being told that he had a brother in a different part of the place, no this was not those terrible people being nice, they told him this the week before his brother died. That was so very cruel of them and you can imagine the effect that this had on him. He was never the same after this, he became so withdrawn. This on top of the the fact that nobody had a smile on their face, we had nothing to smile about, often when I think of that place I remember the vacant look on the boy's face, that vacant look haunts me to this day.

"It took me and the others that I have kept in touch with a long time to deal with what is essentially something that you wouldn't normally think about, you would ignore, you wouldn't give it a passing thought it was just the way it is. We were forced to eat the foul food that was quite literarily and unceremoniously thrown in front of us, you wouldn't dare say anything, and if you did the beatings would make sure that you never opened your mouth again. If you ate it and were sick, the evil, evil bastards would make you eat what you had thrown up. This happened on more than one occasion and I can remember forcing myself not to join in and be sick with the rest, which was hard.

"I believe as a result of the upbringing in that hateful place, many if not all of the boys left that place severely emotionally disturbed, this was to plague them for the rest of their lives. There was never any nice emotion shown to any of them and many were in fact scarred for life through severe sexual abuse and constant physical torture and torment. During this time there was even sexual abuse against the younger ones by some of the older boys in this place and I know now that this was because the nuns did everything they could to oppress the natural order of things. This in its turn forced some of the older boys to take out their sexual urges on the younger ones, doing things to some of the younger ones in the woods. I blame this squarely on the way they had been brought up by some of these evil women the *Sisters of Charity*."

CHAPTER TWENTY THREE
A BAND OF BROTHERS

THE private members' club in the centre of Newcastle was owned and run by Michael Sayers, a member of one of the most well-known and well-respected families in Newcastle. I had done little bits of work with several members of Michael's family from the 1960s to the 1990s and several of his family had come to me seeking advice, which was freely given. I was quite overwhelmed, and very grateful, when I told Michael I was arranging a reunion for some of the old boys from the St Mary's Orphanage in Tudhoe, County Durham: he offered the use of one of the rooms in his club free of charge, and the first round of drinks on the house.

A lot of research had been done and quite a bit of memory searching by some of the first Tudhoe old boys I had been in touch with, not least Ken Young, who was able to draw up a list of many of the boys who would have been in the orphanage at the same time as us, and a list of names of most of the Sisters of Charity there at the time and others members of staff who had made our young lives hell. It has to be said that some of the Sisters and staff did not take part in the cruelty and beatings meted out to the boys, but the majority did. In the minority, and these people were very much the exception, there were Sisters and staff who never struck a boy in anger; but they witnessed the beatings and said nothing and that made them as guilty as the sadistic bullies who took perverted pleasure in seeing the boys in pain and in tears. There was the odd member of staff, again very much the exception, who were actually kind to the boys, but they could be counted on one hand.

The research leading up to the big reunion night had taken many months and some of the old boys had enlisted the help of their computer-literate sons and daughters, or even grandchildren, to help track down some of the old boys via the internet. Many were still alive, many still living in the North East, but others were scattered over the length and breadth of Britain. As we were all now in our late sixties, and some even in their early seventies, it was inevitable that the researchers had found that some of the old boys were now dead. There were others that had been tracked down who didn't want their names associated with the reunion – or included in this book – for family reasons. It appeared these men had mental scars from their time in the home that ran so deep they wanted to bury their dark memories well in the past. Or perhaps they had not even told their families about their horrendous treatment at the hands of the Roman Catholic sadistic perverts? Who knows? I felt sorry for them, but not as sorry for the old boys that I knew for sure were now living life like hermits in their own homes, frightened to go out, and those that had, since their time in the home, taken their own lives.

On one hand I felt proud to have helped organise this reunion night, but on the other I was rather nervous about meeting some of the men who I had never seen or spoken to for more than 50 years – yes, for more than half a century! It was amazing, and somewhat humbling, to realise that many had agreed to come along to the night, some from hundreds of miles away, despite the awful memories it may rekindle for them. Would it be painful for them to relive those horrific times? Would they feel comfortable talking about what happened, or would they clam up, preferring to remember only some of the good things about the home? It is well known that the worst memories of childhood are the easiest to suppress, the easiest to bury deep, deep, into the sub-conscious mind.

In my best suit and tie and well-polished shoes I stood at the bar with a pint in my hand. In a corner of the room Michael Sayers had provided a nice buffet for the old boys, again all free of charge. I wondered what the night would go like, and how many would turn up, but it turned out I had nothing to worry about because several of the old boys turned up to reminisce.

This was an informal gathering of a band of men who had last seen each other just as teenage boys in the 1950s. As they each walked into the room, some more quietly than others, I recognised a lot of their faces, despite the years that had passed. It was strange, but in the man I could see the boy. The faces were obviously older, the eyes more lined and tired, but there was the recognition, and not just the physical recognition of a face you had seen before or a voice you had heard, but the almost spiritual recognition that we had all been on a collective journey in our boyhood, a journey that was full of violence, indoctrination and fear. And this meant there was a bond between us, a bond so strong it had not been broken even by the passage of five decades. It felt like we were a band of old soldiers who had been through the horrors of war and we were meeting up for the last time, before we shuffle off this mortal coil, to discover the truth of our time spent in St Mary's Orphanage and whether or not our memories of that time really did evoke the nightmare we believed it was.

Tommy Little, Tommy Warner, Joe McClarence, Mario, Joe Thompson

As the drink flowed, the ice was broken and we old boys sat around a table supping our pints, initially trying to recollect the names of some of the boys we could remember. The sparks between us meant we were able to sweep the cobwebs from our minds. Soon we were able to come up with a list of some of the names, others we could only remember a first name, a surname or a nickname, but everyone had stories to tell. Among the names we dragged from the 1950s into 2009 were my good mate Harry Marsden, who had died only recently, brothers Joe and Kenny Young, Peter Sample, David Brown, the Boyes brothers, William Sinnet, Bob Fairley, Brian and Michael Sloan, Brian Manderville, Bobby Richardson, Tommy Bolam and his brother John, David Crookshanks, Douglas Cranston, Matthew Leymouth, Ronnie and Robert Smith, Jimmy and Wilfy Butler, a lad called Flannigan and another called Brannigan, whose first names unfortunately escaped us, the Seery brothers, John Doyle and "Clagger" Conroy and many, many more.

Johnny Starr a good friend of Mario

Even the names of the Sisters of Mercy resurfaced, mainly thanks to Ken Young. There was Sister Monica, Sister Helen, Sister Kevin (all mother superiors) Sisters Patricia, Francis, Lucy, Veronica, Philomena, Mary, Ann, Teresa, Catherine, Brennan, Angela, and two by the name of Sister Louise, Sister Pat and Sister Josie.

Staff workers we recalled included Tommy Hall, a heating engineer and gardener, Tom Donnelly, who was also a gardener, Mr Rutherford, a joiner, Mr Simon and Peter Garrity, all Masters in the seniors, Kitty Wear, Molly Malone, Miss Elizabeth, Mrs Buff and Mary Bowman.

"They weren't all bad," said Ken Young.

"All as bad as each other," I said. "Because even if they didn't beat us lads, they knew about it and did nothing."

Ken Young, who spent eight years at St Mary's and who left in 1952, said: "Granted, it was a terrible place. I remember Tom Donnelly, I got a good whipping off him for running away from the home. My shirt was taken off my back and I was held over the chair by two of the nuns while he laid into me with a bamboo cane. He wasn't even a teacher, he was a bloody gardener, and they allowed him and helped him to do that to me! It beggars belief really."

"It was a closed environment," I said. "They could do anything they wanted to us and we could do fuck all about it. I told the police what was going on loads of times, but they just chucked us back in there and left us to look after ourselves. We were only young boys, for fuck sake!"

Some of the old boys raised their eyebrows when I raised my voice and swore, but I was angry at the injustice of it all, and they all knew what I was talking about because they had all been through it.

Ken said: "John Doyle and Clagger Conroy got the same beating after we were on the run for three days. When we got back to school we had another caning. Even the bloody boiler man punched me in the eyes for nothing – the bloody boiler man! I nearly lost my eyes because of him. He also tried to assault me in the toilet, trying to pull my trousers down, but I fought like a tiger and kicked him in the balls and I jumped over the door."

Quiet laughter rippled through the gathered men, amused by the thought of a cruel member of staff getting a good kicking in the goolies.

"It wasn't funny at the time," Ken said, who couldn't also help but laugh. "The bugger was in his forties, he shouldn't have been hitting bloody little kids."

Everyone nodded their heads in agreement.

"What about the weapons they used to use on us?" I asked. "The birch, the cat o nine tails. Those were things they used on grown men locked up in jails for awful crimes, yet they used the same on us."

Ken said: "The nuns would lash us over the head with their Rosary Beads. Can you imagine that, beads they were meant to pray with used as a flaming weapon?"

"I can remember being constantly hungry," said Ken. "The food was bloody terrible and I used to go looking for scraps of bread they'd thrown out for the chickens. I used to even eat raw bloody cooking apples that I'd nicked, even though they made my guts ache."

Ken said: "One of the staff, Mary Bowman, was in charge of the bread room. She had a few fingers missing which she had sliced off accidentally with the bread slicer. She caught me in the bread room stealing a piece of crust and she laid me out with a ladle. On the way to school I used to pick orange peel, apple gowks or even chewed gum from the gutter and eat it.

"I remember Sister Francis, the only decent one of the lot. Me, my brother and Conroy got caught nicking some sweets out of her cupboard. She let us off but we had to kneel on the floor and beg forgiveness."

"Forgiveness, they should be turning in their graves asking for our forgiveness," I said. "That whole bloody praying thing in front of the Virgin Mary. Can you remember that? And going to Mass and Benediction and saying the Rosary all the time and reading the Catechism. No wonder we painted the bloody Virgin Mary black. Can you remember that?"

All the old boys burst into laughter. "You should have seen their faces! I thought some of the Sisters were going to have a heart attack!" Said John.

"But you and your mate paid the price, didn't you John?" I nodded my head in sadness, remembering the pain.

"Do you remember when we had to go to confession and tell our sins?" asked Ken. "I told the priest, Father Oswald, who we nicknamed Ozzie Pie, that I had swiped some pears out of his orchard. He didn't tell me to say four Hail Marys, he just ran out of the bloody confession box and clouted me across the ears. So much for bloody forgiveness!"

Again there was howls of laughter, not at the thought of Ken getting a clout, just the way he recollected the story and told it.

"What about the bloody farmer who came into the home wanting us to slave for him in his fields, picking spuds and turnips?" asked Ken. "He would walk up and down the field with a big stick and lash us over the back, telling us to get the sacks of spuds on to the trailer. At the end of the day he would bring out a bucket of cocoa which was just made with hot water, no milk and no sugar. Then he'd give us a lift on the back of his trailer to the home, and it was always bloody freezing on the back of that trailer. We used to sing on the way back: *Down, down Tiplings, down on Tiplings Farm, you work all day, you get no pay, but you get black cocoa if you stay, down on Tiplings Farm*".

"The farmer once thrashed one of the lads for letting his trailer's tyres down with a stick but he went too far. We all shouted

"*Woe, for nowt! Woe, for nowt!*", which we always shouted when one of the lads was beaten badly. We threw the bucket of cocoa over him and ran off in all directions into the woods, dreading the time we'd have to go back to the home."

"We've all got some bad memories of the fucking place," I said. "Even Christmas was crap. I remember they invited a Press photographer in and a photo was published of us all supposedly happy, looking forward to the big day. It was all a bloody con so that they could get more donations."

"There were some good times, John, but just a few," said Ken.

"I can't fucking remember any."

"Well, can you remember our trip to Seaton Carew on the coast?" Ken asked. "We'd look forward to it and count the days and the nuns would make us pray for sunny weather. If it rained we didn't go but if we did go we would sing "*for he's a jolly good fellow*" to the driver and once there the nuns would have a word with the fairground owner and they took pity on us and gave us free rides. For me it was an adventure, like getting out of prison. It felt like, for that one time of the year, we were free."

"Then it was back to the misery and the beatings. The tasteless food, living in fear during the night, then marching to fucking school in the morning with everyone gawping at us as if we'd just come out of the zoo," I said.

Ken said: "The marches to school. I remember them. There was a poor lad who had one leg shorter than the other and when we were marched to school he had to put one leg on the pavement and another in the gutter, just so he could walk level."

The old boys laughed so much at that, some had tears rolling down their cheeks.

"You might think it's funny now, but that was bloody child cruelty," said Ken, then adding: "There was another woman, much older than the rest, Miss Gibbs they called her. She had white hair and she didn't like the way we were treated. I met her in Sunderland one day in 1989 when I was with a mate of mine. When I told her I was in the home where she worked, she broke down and cried. She said she didn't know how we survived and how she had prayed for us."

"But she done fuck all to stop it!" I said.

One of the old boys listening in, laughing when we laughed, and supping his pint was John Bolem. He had been pretty quiet most of the night so I asked him his thoughts. John had been placed in the home in 1948 at the age of ten for nicking one shilling and sixpence, hardly a major crime.

"At the time I was living in a miserable old tenement building on Westmorland Road in Newcastle. The flat had only two rooms for the whole family: my mother, father, brother and sister and me. Times were really tough and if I could escape I would hot foot it down to the town, often just to escape the place. It was just such a day as that, when my friend and I found ourselves down at the Central Station. I often remember all the hustle and bustle of the town, and of course there was always lots of people coming and going.

"I was a ten year old boy who was totally out of control. I saw a lady walking by with a nice ladies handbag which obviously was going to have some cash in it, and the inevitable happened: I stole it. Inside the bag there was one and six pence, this was just enough money for us to take ourselves off to the cinema in Gateshead. We had a great day but reality struck on the way home when we were picked up by the police, it was late at night and we were on our own, with pennies and halfpennies in our pockets. The police sharp got it out of my pal that I had stolen the ladies handbag. I was only a kid but that didn't stop them from locking me up for the night in the cells in Pilgrim Street Police Station. Over the coming weeks the authorities kept a watchful eye on me and I was running wild in the streets, so when it eventually came to the time I had to go to the Juvenile Court I was again locked up in a cell, with all these older men around me.

"They didn't give me a chance and I was first sent to a remand home to stay there while awaiting my fate. Two weeks later the terrible and awful nightmare began, that was the day I first entered St Mary's Orphanage. The first night there was to turn out to be an eventful one, just as the lights were going out, the eleven-year-old 'Daddy' of the dormitory thought he would give me a good hiding. But he obviously didn't realize that I was a tough street kid and so I showed all the kids in the dorm who was boss as I gave him a hiding."

All the old boys sat intently listening to John. His memories were painful.

"The punishments and the cruelty in the place would often lead me to go on the run in a feeble attempt to find something better.

This would often spur me to gather a few of the lads together, Mario being one of them. We would then try and find our way home. Even if this was bad in our minds, it was definitely a lot better than being in that terrible place constantly in fear of beatings by the nuns and staff who basically treated us worse than their dogs and cats.

"One time we ran and ran and, crazy as it may sound, we thought that we must have gone at least as far as London, our feet were killing us and we were freezing cold. We got ourselves bedded down in a haystack. It was so cold Mario had wet himself..."

"Did I fuck!" I interjected.

"You did," said John. "You were only a kid and it was bloody freezing. We didn't want to stop running. With the cold Mario's pants had ice in them and he was shivering like hell. But in the early hours of the morning, we had a rude awakening when the police surrounded us and we were kicked and marched back to St Mary's Orphanage. We had only been three miles away from the home, but it felt like hundreds to us. At this time I had a shock of curly hair and one of the punishments for our escape was to have our head shaved, so the rest of the kids knew who had tried to run away, they also made us wear the dreaded red jumper, which the nuns would make us wear as a sign of our shame.

"One day, I couldn't believe my eyes, there in front of me was my brother Thomas. He was eighteen months older than me, but he was not really a bad lad, he did not know what he'd let himself in for with this place and I remember a feeling of horror and shock going through my mind in what I knew about the place and how it was going to affect him. He hated the place the same as everyone else and also just as badly wanted to go home. I was still, even after the horrible things that happened to me in St Mary's, without any fear and wanted to help him get out. I stole Nun Molly Malone's purse and gave Thomas the money to get himself home. Again, though, we didn't get far. I will never forget the punishment, this time it was the birch, administered by Joe Donnelly who was the maintenance man, this sick bastard really enjoyed his work and I am not talking about the maintenance.

"The head Nun stood over us as the blows rained down on our bare backsides. She just stood there without any expression and without any feelings. We were in agony afterwards and we could not sit down for over a week. I was still very young, but I must say, that place knocked all the fear and feeling out of me for a long time, even now I remember it all. I met lads in there who came from all over the country and every one of them to a man can tell a different horror story about that terrible place. My brother for years had a thing about toilet paper or should I say the lack of it, at St Mary's: when you used the toilets there was never any paper, you had to wipe your back-side with your hand and then rub your hand down the wall. We called it 'coiting'. This nightmare, every-thing about the home, still haunts me to this day.

Mario relaxing on holiday .

John looked up from his pint and saw that we were all looking at him. It seemed he was a little embarrassed bearing his soul like that. But we all felt his pain, because we had all shared the same horrendous experiences. If those things had happened today or even in the 1980s, there would have been a Government enquiry and heads would have rolled.

For a moment the room went quiet. Then Ken Young lightened the mood: "Do you remember Tip the dog? It would follow us all over, to school and then wait for us coming out. When we started singing a certain song the dog would start howling as if it was singing."

The old boys smiled.

"There was one time during a summer all we lads were told to line up in the courtyard and this posh couple came along the line inspecting us," said Ken. "I remember it was Christmas time. Anyway this couple picked me out and took me to their house in Whitley Bay for a week. For one whole week I wasn't hit or shouted at and when I told the woman how badly we were treated in the home she cried. She asked me to put a stocking out on Christmas Eve and I asked her what for. She asked if we didn't do this in the home, and I said no, we got nothing. For that one week

189

my belly was always full, with the kind of food I had never seen before, never mind eaten. But the thing is, I wanted to go back to the home, I didn't want to stay in Whitley Bay.

"Why the hell did you want to go back there?" I asked.

"Because I missed you lot," said Ken, a genuine tear starting to roll down his reddened cheek. "There was a great camaraderie amongst us boys, probably because we were all in the same boat, suffering the same beatings, hunger and verbal abuse," said Ken, who was now quite emotional.

"In a way it glued us together, made us stronger. We looked after each other. In my eyes we weren't bad kids just because we'd been abandoned by our parents, or sent away. We didn't deserve the punishment we got. But that whole experience, that whole damned childhood, made us friends, real friends. Really, we were a band of brothers."

For a few moments silence fell upon all of us. And the eyes of all the old boys present, all mostly hard men and street-fighters of the past, glistened with wetness.

I raised my glass: "To the band of brothers," I said.

"To the band of brothers!" said the old boys in unison.

CHAPTER TWENTY FOUR

THE MAN WITH NO PAST

SIXTY seven years had passed since I had been found as an infant neglected and abused in a terraced slum on the outskirts of Bishop Auckland, County Durham, which led to me being put in care and my parents both being jailed for six months with hard labour for child neglect. Near the end of 2008, nearly seven decades later, and for many that's a lifetime, something happened which I never thought possible ... I was reunited with the older brother I had heard about but thought I would never see.

I had been talking over the years with my other brothers and sisters about our past and our harsh upbringing and the name Harry S had been mentioned a few times, but the details were so sketchy we couldn't pinpoint exactly who Harry S was. Then my sister started doing a bit of research on the internet and discovered Harry S was indeed my older brother and not just that, that his family, too, were trying to trace his family history.

One thing led to an other and a reunion was planned in Newcastle, with Harry S and his family travelling up from where they lived in Aylesbury, Buckinghamshire, to a hotel not far from where I live. I had spoken to Harry S on the telephone before the meeting and simply said: "Hello Harry. It's John, your brother." I had always been the type to get straight to the point. He appeared delighted to have heard from me.

Harry was now 71 and he had lived a full life never knowing who he really was or where he was from. He was married to Linda with two children and a grandson and he had memories of a childhood in care but, other than his time with foster parents and joining the Merchant Navy, the details were vague. He had thought about his childhood often but it was only now, before it was too late, that something was being done about it. He was a man with no real past.

The lot of us got together over a celebratory drink at the Novotel in Kenton Bar, just across the road from my house. The Press were there and we made the news in the North East and in Aylesbury, both in the newspapers and on television and in a national magazine. It was such an unusual story and when it came

191

to light hundreds of people I knew and others in the North East were talking about it. It attracted the most hits on the website of the regional newspaper, The Sunday Sun, such was its popularity.

Harry, Mario & Frankie at the Novotel.

Apart from the fact that we had never seen each other since we were babies, the most striking thing was what different lives we had led. Harry was put into the care of the Barnardo's charity where he was looked after well. For Harry it was a childhood experience totally opposite to the childhood I had endured at St Mary's Orphanage in Tudhoe, County Durham. He had never been beaten or abused and later in his life he was placed with foster parents in Fincham, Norfolk, where he was also treated well and made friends with two other children in the same foster home who became just like his family.

When Harry left Barnardo's he joined the Merchant Navy, something the charity had prepared him for, and travelled the world. When he had to leave the Merchant Navy because of an illness he managed to get other jobs and ended up as a manager at an engineering firm. The only crime he had ever committed in his life was driving three miles an hour above a 30mph speed limit.

At the hotel when I first met Harry I could see he was smaller than me, like me smartly dressed, like me a smoker and, like me, he still had a full head of hair. When we looked at each other we knew that we were brothers. Harry had a different father to me, but we had both come from the same womb, so to me that made us brothers.

Harry and his family had done some further research into his childhood and his background and had managed to get hold of a Barnardo's report which read: "The mother's husband was lazy. He ill treated the mother and Harry and said that the trouble was caused by the presence of Harry in their home. There were constant quarrels because he said Harry was having food that his own child should have and that he ate too much. He often beat the boy, who was terrified when he was in the house."

I couldn't help thinking that discovering what he had about his childhood must have been a terrible blow to Harry, but his reaction was one of stoicism. He was quite philosophical about it all. Harry wasn't bothered that me, his brother, had been involved in heavy crime much of his life. One of the most poignant and true things Harry said was: "I believe the way we have turned out is all down to which children's homes we were sent to. It could all have been so different."

Another child mentioned was our baby sister, but she never survived to go with Harry. She was dead on arrival at the institution. Catherine was her name. The records and newspaper show that the authorities were trying to prosecute the parents, but for some unknown reason they were never prosecuted, however the parents were kept under "observation". My family and I were aware that we did have an older brother and sister, we were also aware that this elder sister had died, that is all we knew and that is the way it stayed for seventy years. It was only recently that my family and I started to get details of what happened to both Harry and Catherine. My brother Robert's wife Cath was scanning through the Internet when by pure chance she came across a seventy year old man who was trying to seek knowledge of his past, that seventy year old pensioner was our very long lost brother Harry.

A man who did not even know that he had brothers and sisters, in fact he did not really know who he was. I feel that when he was younger he in some way coped with the situation, but it was when he got older and married it was then that he would have been haunted by the question of who he was. It must have been diffi-cult for him, wondering all that time who he was and were he had come from, what his roots were; after all it's only human nature to ask these questions and I am sure I would have been asking them as well. His wife must have wondered who he really was, where had this man come from, especially when they were about to get married and spend the rest of their lives together, the man she was going to bear children too. One can only imagine the surreal and unimaginable situation the man with no past found himself in, questions would come from his wife and then ulti-mately his children about his past that he could not answer; his children must have thrown questions at him. Daddy have you got a mother, a father, brothers or sisters? Why have we not got a grandma like other children? In essence, what his wife and chil-dren were saying to him is "Daddy who are you?" One can only imagine the psychological and emotional damage this extremely unfortunate man has had to endure through no fault of his own making.

It is truly a terrible blow that fate had bestowed upon this man, as I am writing this I cannot deny that for possibly the first time in my life I feel very emotional and struggling to hold back the tears, as I am now at the age of sixty seven coming to realize and coming to terms with what can only be described as a tragic and almost unbelievable horror story, one that has befell all of us in our family. When I have put this into writing myself, word for word, I am myself on a horrific and emotional roller-coaster ride that I have never known before, and I can only ask the question why? Well I can only imagine that for all Harry and his family, his wife and two girls, that making contact they would be extremely apprehensive at the thought of meeting us all: the family they had not know even existed. I can understand that in essence Harry S is a man coming in from the wilderness after seventy years. I had thought the meeting might have been too much for him to take.

A remarkable thing happened, during the time the internet research was going on, which can only be described as a monu-mental twist of fate. My brother Robert and his wife went on a holiday to Egypt in the Middle East. At this time Harry's wife Linda was in seriously ill in hospital. Whilst on holiday my brother Robert and his wife met other English holidaymakers and one of these lived in the same town as my brother Harry. During a conversation it turned out that this woman they were talking too was a nurse, not only was she a nurse, but she was the very nurse who cared for Harry's wife Linda. Now that's got to be more than a million to one chance, it is almost spooky. When the nurse got back home to England she told Harry who was visiting his wife in hospital that she had met and had been talking to his brother Robert. I was not there, but one can only imagine the shock he got on hearing such news, it was then that all the apprehension he must have been feeling obviously disappeared. Harry almost immediately phoned Robert, which was the very first time he had spoken to another member of his family, his own flesh and blood. Harry told Robert that when the nurse told him of the extraordinary meeting he felt that it was meant to be, that he must come to see us in Newcastle, he said that it is fate for him to come home after seventy years. I myself and all of my family were both ecstatic and delighted that after all this time our very long lost brother was coming in from the wilderness. I have never really believed in miracles, but this extraordinary chance meeting in Egypt can only be described as a miracle, one that was meant to be.

CHAPTER TWENTY FIVE

IS IT NATURE OR IS IT NURTURE?

"GIVE me a boy until he is seven and I'll show you the man".

The saying was formulated by the Jesuit religious order, Society of Jesus – a Roman Catholic order founded by Saint Ignatius of Loyola in 1534 to defend Catholicism against the Reformation and to do missionary work among the heathens. The Jesuits were strongly committed to education and scholarship and, as I found to my costs, indoctrination of the highest order.

The philosophy, despite it being the tenet of an ancient religious order, had permeated mainstream Catholicism down the ages and obviously saw it's way into all Catholic churches, schools, and in my case, orphanages for those kids whose parents had abandoned them.

Me and my brother Harry S were from the same womb with only four years difference in our ages. Yes, he had a different father to me, but nevertheless we carried the same genes inherited from our mother, we were born in the same place and we were each put into care at a very young age having been neglected by our parents.

We shared a bond that is generally viewed as the most common and strong bond you can get, we were of the same blood; blood relations. So, nature would have it, that from our very conception we would be destined to share similar character traits, similar physical characteristics, even perhaps, our destinies would be intertwined.

And yet over a period of almost 70 years we grew up to become very different men; Harry S a respectable family man, who, apart from a speeding ticket, had never transgressed the law and me a top villain in Northern England with a deeply ingrained hatred for all in authority and a burning desire, because of my childhood, for revenge.

By the age of seven Harry S had been in one or two Barnardo's homes and was then placed with a foster family, sharing his life with foster parents and two other young children who became his family. He didn't know who his real family was. By the time I was seven, if I had any normality left in my bones it had been beaten out of me by my Roman Catholic tormentors who wanted to shape me into the person they wanted me to be.

They wanted me to work hard, that was pretty obvious, and they wanted me to obey the law and the rules, attend church and confession, be dutiful, respectful of authority, charitable, honest and forgiving. In essence they wanted to mould me into a man of religiousness and righteousness. They failed, miserably, not just in my case but in many hundreds of others.

What the powers-that-be in the orphanage didn't understand is that you might be able to beat a dog into submission, but it's very different with a human being, particularly for those at a raw, tender and vulnerable age such as children.

What I can't understand is why? Why all the physical and mental torture on innocent bodies and minds whose only "crime" was the crime of their parents in neglecting or abandoning them? Surely these young people needed the best care and support that could be offered to them, and a good education. Like a young plant a caring gardener wants to nurture, they needed to be allowed to grow in the right environment.

When Harry S left care, he wasn't really looking for a family, he had one in the shape of his foster parents and the two other foster children he grew up with and kept in touch with them for the rest of his life.

When I left care I was looking for a family, because I had never had one. There was no emotional support given to me and the hundreds of other lads in the orphanage and other orphanages by the staff; the kind of emotional support you would get from a family.

So I got into crime, inevitably ended up in borstal, then jail, and all the time I was looking for people I could make a connection with, with whom I shared some common ground and even character traits. I found my family in the criminal underworld; like-minded brothers and sisters with the same outlook on life as me, who wanted to beat the system and grab what they could. And I became very good at crime, earning a very decent living, travelling the country and meeting many very interesting characters.

Harry S lived an honest life. He earned an honest living, married and had children and grandchildren and lived in a pleasant house in suburbia. He had enjoyed his life and told me he wouldn't have changed a thing, though news of his very early childhood when he was abandoned came as a shock to him.

I've enjoyed my life, apart from the illness I have suffered. I was a very successful criminal and, mainly thanks to my planning, professionalism and my capacity to know when a job might be risky, I have never spent time in a long-term prison.

Just one question remains. If Harry S had been placed in St Mary's Orphanage, Tudhoe, County Durham, and I had been placed in a Barnardo's home then later foster care, how would we boys have turned out?

The answer probably lies in the opening statement of this chapter: "Give me a boy until he is seven, and I'll show you the man."